TRUST AN
ENGLISHMAN

TRUST AN ENGLISHMAN

JOHN KNOWLER

HARCOURT BRACE JOVANOVICH, INC.

NEW YORK

ISBN 0-15-191317-X
Library of Congress Catalog Card Number: 72-93147
First American edition
B C D E

Contents

Introduction

The Anglo-Saxon likes to argue *a posteriori*, from the bottom upward, from practical experience. It is the tradition of Bacon and Newton.

> Harold Macmillan, 1950

One could almost say that while the French are divided *between* themselves, the English are divided *within* themselves.

> Claude Lévi-Strauss, 1970

The American radical Irving Howe has described those Americans who grew up in the United States during the last war as 'the generation that did not show up'. I think the same could be said for us, their British contemporaries. A generation, born in the 'twenties, fought the war. The children of the 'forties grew into the first post-war generation. Those of us born in the 'thirties did not seem to do anything. We disappeared. Whenever the roll has been called, we have been absent. This book is an attempt to own up about where we, some of us at least, have been.

In a nation of individualists no one can claim too seriously to be typical. But the range of my experience seems to me peculiarly English. By negative identification, claiming in no way to be extraordinary, I do imagine myself to be unusually typical. And a faceless generation has a heritage: so I am proposing myself as witness not only for a generation but in some ways also for an entire nation. As an autobiography, this is a random piece of work. The events are such as might happen any day to anyone. I mean them to illustrate this typically English life, and at the same time to demonstrate some of the qualities of Englishness and to suggest how these might be rooted in history.

My own education left me ignorant of all history later than the Second Punic War (219–202 B.C.). I have had to read in order to support, or disprove, what was no more than my instinctive sense of the past. Most direct quotations I have attributed, but I am indebted for their ideas to more authors than I could list without a spurious air of scholarship. If they happen to read what I have written and recognize its origin in their own remarks, I hope they will understand that I am a grateful and respectful thief. And I do not forget that, every time I make use of secondary sources, I take advantage of someone else's industry.

As to my own story, I have tried to do so, but I cannot swear that I have always told the truth: memory is elusive, and I have not checked on it. This is not simple idleness. I wanted to preserve my own sense of what had influenced me, and what I remembered as the truth seemed more important than the facts. That also gave me the excuse to present a view of things as I see them. Intentionally I have kept this as spontaneous as the labour of writing a book will allow. I wanted not to lose that part of the book that is in a sense unintentionally revealing: in relating an English experience, in discussing English qualities, I hope I might have revealed my own English attitudes, not evident to me, but apparent to a reader.

A nation is a collection of individuals, but it has an identity of its own. Both the nation and the individuals share a common history. Both react psychologically in terms of that past. Yet the concept of nationality diminishes, and already there is a sense in which I am an Englishman and my son is not. I hope this book might explain to his children something of the mystery of what being English used to be.

1. John Bull and Jack Beaver

A nation fond of their liberty, learned, witty, despising
life and death, a nation of philosophers; ... by God,
English wisdom and honesty is above yours.

Voltaire, 1726

He had an English look; that is, was square
In make, of a complexion white and ruddy.

Byron, Don Juan (1824)

What is the size of England?
About 430 miles long and 320 broad.
What is the climate of England?
Moist but healthy.
What is the character of the English people?
Brave, intelligent and very persevering.

from a school textbook, 1870

I neither like nor understand the English, except after
they are dead.

François Mauriac (1885–1970)

My grandfather was the publican of The Green Man.* I never knew him, but my imaginary portrait is quite clear: a Victorian paterfamilias, a larger-than-life figure, portly and whiskered, with that somewhat congested vitality, swearing like a trooper, dominating his family and his long-suffering wife with racing, confident selfishness. If he came across one of his household momentarily idle, he wanted to know why they were not usefully employed. The day her mother died Auntie Phyll went out and bought a trunk: Auntie Edie had made her escape already into marriage, and Phyll did not think she could tolerate life as the remaining daughter of this monstrous father. But she did not leave. She carries the marks of that spiritual domination still.

Grandfather was well known in the town, presiding in the bar of the pub — in those days the landlord did not himself serve drinks — or setting off to the races in his pony and trap. His rages were legendary. My father would recall him with affectionate admiration, but with evident relief that he was free of his domination. Once, before they were married, my mother came by train to visit my father. She was surprised that he met her at the station, even more that my grandfather had lent him his car. Indeed, she began to grow suspicious when my father insisted that they take a ride round before they went home. Later she discovered that my grandfather wanted her kept out of the way while he carried out a delicate negotiation: he had got the maid into trouble, and her mother had come to demand compensation. No doubt in those days there was a recognized

* Robin Hood, in Lincoln green.

price on virtue. If family legend is to be believed, there was a succession of these living-in maids, and as many mothers to be placated.

I don't remember the man, but I do remember his funeral. I was too young to attend, and I was held up to the window of my room at the top of my father's house as the funeral cars drew away. From above the people were insignificant, moving, it seemed, through a sea of flowers. That is another legend: so well known was my grandfather in the town that the wreaths filled every ground-floor room of the house, occupying the floors, chairs, tables, every flat surface, and still spilling out on to the lawn behind.

That grandfather was unknown, but he plays an important role for me. He is my own John Bull: 'ruddy and plump, with a pair of cheeks like a trumpeter ... an honest, plain-dealing fellow, choleric, bold, and of a very inconstant temper ... loving his bottle and his diversion: for to say truth, no man kept a better house than John, nor spent his money more generously.'* For three centuries that Fal-staffian figure was our own idea of the typical Englishman. He was not necessarily viewed with much affection. In the nineteenth century he was often seen as a blockhead, crude, unimaginative, pigheaded and something of a fool—but, like my grandfather, recollected with a certain warmth. When, in 1940, Winston Churchill needed to unite the country behind him, he deliberately affected a John Bull manner, with glowering looks, pugnacious speeches, an English inability to master foreign words. He scorned 'asses who speak about *Le Havre*. Havre'—he rhymed it with 'carver'—'it is to any decent man.' Pétain he pronounced 'peetayne'...This was the only identity the British had for themselves. They loved Churchill as they might

---

* John Bull seems to have been invented by Dr John Arbuthnot (this is his description) in a political pamphlet circulated in the London coffee-houses in 1712. But the concept of a true British character, as opposed to the 'foreign' blood of Anglo-Saxons and Normans, had grown with the ascendance of the House of Tudor in the sixteenth century.

love an old bulldog. But it was already an out-of-date idea, the fancy of a rural, underdeveloped nation.

A nation's personality, as much as an individual's, contains elements of disguise, pretending to strength where it knows itself weakest. Alongside English Bullishness has always run the opposite thread: the reserved, polite, diffident Englishman. 'The true English style,' Jane Austen —herself the most English of novelists—called it, 'burying under a calmness that seems all but indifference, the real attachment'. Boisterous John Bull has another side: gentle Jack Beaver, quiet, industrious, tending his island home. Opposites have always co-existed in the British nature. As a nation we have been both Roman and Greek—soldiers and philosophers, Puritans and sensualists. The world admires us for our good manners; Hitler admired our brutality. King Arthur is our hero-king, chivalrous and brutal at the same time, gentleness tempering violence in the famous English compromise. Somewhere in those areas lies the seed of our unhappy reputation for dishonesty.

If my grandfather was John Bull, my father was Jack Beaver. He believed in work, in the intrinsic merit of it. If he stopped working, he was uneasy. The garage that was his business was alongside the house, and he did not keep business hours. Even in the house there was always some task that needed to be done—a room to be painted, apples to be picked. On Sunday mornings when I, with somewhat pretentious ideas of civilized behaviour, would have liked to sit over breakfast with the newspaper, he would move us all by getting up from the table, insisting quietly, 'There's jobs to be done.' What he had in mind was, say, to sweep up outside the back door, or clear out the shed, or hoe weeds from the paths of packed gravel that served our acre of garden, or cut the hedges. We had a gardener, and my father was no expert, but he knew one thing better than 'old Barnard': trees and plants of all varieties benefit from heavy pruning.

My father never had a leisure problem. He never allowed himself leisure. Even if we 'went out' on a Sunday afternoon, and drove to the country and parked the car in a gateway for a couple of hours, he would take with him copies of the *Autocar* and try to catch up with his reading. When he was employing fifty or sixty men, he would still himself go out into the yard at the weekends and sweep the workshops, scattering sawdust from a bucket to absorb the oil.

And every night, after tea, he would bring out his paperwork and sit at the dining-table, with its green, plush cloth balding at the corners, and check through the worksheets and job-cards, and pencil draft letters in his sloping hand on the backs of envelopes. 'ITMA' ('It's That Man Again') was on the wireless. The whole country was listening. It was the Royal Family's favourite programme, we all knew that. When Mrs Mop put her head round the door and said to Tommy Handley, 'Can I do you now, sir?', King George VI and the princesses up there in Buckingham Palace shared the joke with us. My mother would be knitting. My brother (older than me) would be out. My sister was in bed. I would half read, half listen. There were always some sweets in the tin up beside the wireless, and we would pass these round. Liquorice Allsorts were my father's favourites. At about ten we would make a cup of tea. My father's head would fall forward, and he would jerk himself awake. As this movement grew more frequent, my mother would 'tch, tch' unhappily. But he did not give up. Often she would go to bed and leave him to finish, and come down later to find him with his head on his arms, asleep across the table. He never got round to retiring. Illness kept him out of the yard for the last couple of years of his life, but even then he had a bed in a window of the house where he could see over the yard, and watch the traffic of vehicles for repair, and the men going to and from the canteen for their breaks.

But his surveillance was not of the Big Daddy type. He expected hard work and high standards, but most of the time he insisted quietly. He was not a delicate man. He would release a rat from a trap into a shed with the dog, and watch the sport. I think the spectacle that most directly gave him pleasure was a 'clean' boxing match. But he was a modest, reserved, private man. At table my mother tried to draw conversation from him, but he scarcely spoke, sometimes not even answering direct questions, working through his food with unhurried deliberation, carefully with knife and fork paring each quarter of tomato out of its skin while we waited painfully for him to finish.

I was scarcely able to talk to him. I think we both thought that 'education' came between us. At school I believe I was ashamed of him. I could not bring myself to write 'Garage Owner' in the space that demanded to know 'Father's Profession'. I hit on what I believed to be an ingenious solution: I called him simply 'Engineer'. But in the last years of his life we both accepted our limited communication, not explicitly, but by understanding affection in long silences and occasional trivial conversation. Only then, and since his death, did I understand the worth of his qualities—his sincerity, his honesty, his perseverance, his modesty, his determination, his kindness. I believe it was those qualities that made him successful, in a trade where they are not common. He was a craftsman. He could put his ear out from the window of a car and quietly diagnose its trouble from the sound of its engine. In those years I was impractical, a dreamer. I could read *The Times* at the age of seven: that was my skill. My brother was the practical type. He could drive a car by the time he was fourteen, make a strong, perfectly jointed hutch for his ferret, was able to break a rabbit's neck. I suppose I reacted from such a formidable competence.

My father's land was an island, bounded by the river on two sides, by the main road and by the featureless wall of the Powder Mills* on the others. Within that perimeter was the house and the yard. They were quite cut off. If we saw a rabbit in the garden we knew that it must have come across the road one night, and it would stay and live off our vegetables until Barnard or my brother shot it.

My mother did not like us going down the yard. It was dirty. It was dangerous, with lorries and cars constantly on the move. But also there were social reasons. She wished that the garage were not so close to the house; association was unavoidable. Originally my father was in partnership with my uncle, and the firm was Knowler Bros. Uncle Tom and Auntie Lily had half the house, and Uncle Tom shared with my father breakdown duties and emergency repairs. The two families even shared their first car—when cars were rarer, and the business was still small—using it on alternate weekends, while the other brother had his 'weekend on' in the yard. When Uncle Tom left, the firm was renamed, from the name of the house, Hazlemere Motor Co. That had a more dignified ring.

On Saturday afternoons and Sunday mornings a few men worked overtime in the yard. The canteen was closed, and we made tea for them in the house in a big white enamel jug. If it was ready before the bell went I might take it down and stand it on the shelf that ran round the fat cast-iron stove in the main workshop. In winter, occasionally, my father would shyly fetch the bottle from the dining-room and add a dash of rum to the jug. 'Drop of China tea, boy?' he would offer the men who were working late. He called

* The ancient Gunpowder Factory, now an experimental research establishment. From one part of our bank we could see the covered barges hauled along its waterways, and that small stretch of the opposite bank was at times patrolled by armed police, with pistols in their belts. The source of much local folklore, it was exciting to us children, and we dared go only so far into its territory in our boat. A typical tale: during World War I the men coming off the evening shift were several times bombed as they left work. It seemed sinister, since no lights were shown—until someone realized that, as soon as they came out, the first thing the men did was light a cigarette, which was forbidden in the factory. The light of so many matches was visible to the pilots who, in those days, bombed by sight. In that war there were fifty-one Zeppelin and fifty-seven aeroplane raids on Britain.

us all 'boy', even my mother and sister sometimes, absent-mindedly.

Even for me, the dedicated enemy of everything mecha-nical, the only boy who ever found trains intolerably dirty and noisy, the yard had some wonderful attractions. The sign-writer, Mr Cross, often came in the evenings or at weekends. I loved to watch him work, resting his hand on the soft-headed drumstick, filling in the letters so confi-dently, forming them as quickly as I might form letters with a pencil, cleverly shading them in perspective so that they seemed stuck on the side of the lorry. In the 'old shop' the oxy-acetylene gun, with a soft blue tongue of flame licking from its nozzle, stood by a tray of dead coals. If you gripped the shaft and squeezed the lever, the flame shot out in a fierce jet. Then, if you turned it down on the coals, you would have a small area glowing red in a few seconds.

Above was the stores, the great weight of all those spare parts supported in the shop below by beams thick as tree-trunks. I liked to go up the steep oily stairs: at the top was a sort of stable door, the bottom half formed into a metal-topped counter on which the parts clattered as the storemen passed them over. The storemen did not mind me mooning about—or if they did they did not say, since I was 'the Guvnor's boy'. There was a different smell up there, a clean smell of new rubber from the tyres. I would take small boxes from the bins, open them and unwrap some shining object from its waxed paper … then replace it. There were ball-bearings, washers, gaskets, bolts, valves, pistons—all the mysterious inner parts of vehicles. Separate from their mechanical function they were beautiful objects. I had the vague desire to employ them in some satisfying, clean, smooth construction. I suppose now I must give that feeling some sexual connotation, but I was not aware of it at the time. Nor was I thinking of actually making up some contraption. Certainly not that. I could not have told you the function of a quarter of the pieces I picked out, and I would not have wanted to spoil them by making a machine out of them. A boy who came home from school once amazed me by the joy with which he picked dirty parts from the debris round the garage incinerator. There in the black oily slag were half-buried metal objects too small to be piled separately for the scrap merchants: odd ball-bearings, ends of wire, split pins, nameless parts. I was too fastidious to poke about in that dirt. I did not think my mother would approve.

In the course of that education that seemed to separate me from my father, I arrived as an undergraduate at Cambridge. Quite early in the first term, the Master of the College asked the first-year men to sherry. His wife, no doubt dismayed by so many unprepossessing boys, fell back on the clichés of English hospitality. 'Ah,' said Lady ——, '*Knowler*. What an unusual name. What part of the country does that come from?' 'I'm not sure,' I said uncertainly. I had the vague feeling—recurrent throughout my life— of being out of place, as if one were expected to own rather a large part of one of the rural counties. 'I believe we are East Anglian yeoman stock.' It's the awful power of people like Lady —— that they can make you say that.

But actually, though I never had the curiosity to pursue my ancestors beyond my grandfather, I do think of East Anglia as my native land and its inhabitants as my people. 'East Anglians', says Ronald Blythe, 'take a puritan pleasure in work. It's work as a virtue and work as a form of identity.'

England amazingly preserves the distinctions of local populations, of regional architecture from local materials, of differing local habits. Even on the motorways, whose chief characteristic is their monotonous lack of character: as you drive north, accents change, and local food appears in the cafeterias—Eccles cakes, custard pies, curd tarts. Yet the whole country is small enough that in one day's driving

you can visualize yourself rising through it, like mercury in
a thermometer, almost from zero to boiling-point.

The Saxons colonized Kent and Essex one thousand
five hundred years ago. With stocky figures, blue eyes,
fair hair and fleshy faces (farther up the coast, Viking blood
produces a taller physique, typically blonder and narrower
in the face), they and the Angles were conscientious
farmers. I have no need of a family tree to know that these
are my ancestors. Physically we are of a type.* King Harold,
the last Saxon king before the Norman Conquest, founded
the monastery on which the local church stands and,
reputedly, is buried there. Garage-owning is not a country
pursuit, and now the town has been devoured by suburbia,
but when my father first set up on his own, between there
and the outskirts of London were ten miles of orchards. He
and my mother were woken every morning by the pattering
of sheep being driven along the road, down the yard, to
graze on the open ground behind the house — land that was
later our 'paddock'. There were farms close by and a
weekly cattle market, which somewhat incongruously survives in a diminished form. My brother became a good
engineer, but he would rather have been a farmer. While he
was still at school he built a sty and kept pigs in the paddock.
As I remember it, we seemed exactly on the border between
town and country — to the north-east the open farmlands
of Essex, and to the south-west the seeping infilling of
suburban London.

Inevitably regionalism grows less rigid. The last war
took people out of their localities and shuffled them with
natives of every part of the country. Television and mass
communication have provided an alternative to the local
dialect. When the car ceases to be a luxury (about 60 per
cent of households in Britain now have cars), even villages
ignored by public transport find themselves connected to

* A family story: My father, being measured for a suit, glanced at the tailor's
notes while he was out of the room. At the foot was written, 'NB Prom. seat.'

the national cultural grid. Even so, local loyalty dies hard. Since I was seven, when I went away to boarding school, I have spent more time away than at home. I never became part of the community in my home town, never used the local library, or made friends with local children. That has given me divided feelings, belonging, yet feeling out of place. Yet I still have a local attachment. I should never, for instance, choose to live south of the Thames.

And local differences do persist; we are not a homogenous race. In the western extremities, in Cornwall, Wales, Ireland and western Scotland, there is *still* a predominant physical type, with reddish hair and freckled skin; and still even, in the Welsh language and Scottish and Irish Gaelic, variations of the original Celtic tongues, brought from Central Europe and carried across England under pressure from the Romans and us Anglo-Saxons. There are Picts in eastern and central Scotland,* Normans knocking about in the south, and the 'other Welsh'—dark Mediterranean people driven to the hills by the Bronze Age Beaker Folk.

Bronze Age! I would expect such considerations to be absurd, but they are not. An English race that spoke neither Anglo-Saxon nor 'Court' French, but a sort of Chaucerian English ('Goddams', Joan of Arc called us already) did not appear until the fourteenth century. This may be the last generation, but local language and local accents do survive. I know a man whose 'r's, a sort of roughened version of the French sound, I took to be a speech defect, until I chanced to discover that he came from a small Northumberland village where that pronunciation, through some accident of history, is universal.

A survey of English dialects has found more than eighty expressions for 'left-handed'. It's hard not to feel senti-

---

* Celts also, but a darker strain. *Picti* (painted) to the Romans, from their tattoo marks. Every schoolboy knows that Hadrian built his wall because he could not conquer these fierce, wiry guerrilla fighters.

mental about the pervasiveness of standard English if it will deprive us of bawky-handed, clicky-handed, coochy-gammy, cow-pawed, cunny-handed, gibble-fisted, kay-neived, kittaghy, scroochy, skiffy, quippy, watty ... Though it is chiefly those of us who do not use the words who regret their passing, and there is in this a hint of patronizing, of nostalgia for the days when the natives used to wear their colourful costumes. But the significance of these quaint regional expressions is their nationality: 'clicky', used in Cornwall, is Celtic in origin. So is 'coochy', found in Devon. 'Car-handed', found in the north-east, is, as it should be, Scandinavian. In our part of the world we used 'cack-handed', which also means clumsy, as these 'left-handed' words usually do. 'Cack' I now discover is Middle English. That's as it should be — Middle English has Anglo-Saxon roots. 'Cack' meant to shit.

The members of my family — aunts, uncles, parents, sister and brother — have all lived within a couple of hours' journey of one another, in Essex, Suffolk, Hertfordshire, Sussex: certainly not in order to be able to visit one another easily, but because it is in the south-east that they feel at home. Two aunts live in Brighton. That is important: every true Englishman has at least one aunt in Brighton. A cousin whose job took him to Yorkshire and Scotland has returned 'home' to the outskirts of London.

On the petrified strata of these ancient invading races, successive waves of refugees have broken. Refugees are passive invaders, and their effect is slowly felt. Dutch and Flemish Protestant weavers, refugees from Catholic perse-cution, settled in East Anglia in the sixteenth century and revitalized the English weaving industry. In the seventeenth century fifty thousand Huguenots fled Louis XIV and forcible Catholicism — a significant proportion in a total population of six million. Seventy years ago one hundred thousand Russians and Eastern Europeans constituted the first wave of Jewish refugees. 'Their standard of manners and living can only be compared with that of a pig,' commented the *Nineteenth Century*. A second wave came in the 'thirties, with the rise of Nazi Germany. Englishmen saw their jobs at risk, and the prospect of their wages being undercut. Perhaps seventy years is too short a time to look for acceptance, on either side. The communities are separate: London, Leeds, Liverpool, Manchester, Glasgow, all have their Jewish neighbourhoods. The only London bus that carries an advertisement for the *Jewish Chronicle* is the bus to Golders Green. For some reason — perhaps because publicans are natural reactionaries — pubs have never liked Jews, neither have Jews liked pubs. It seems the exclusion is mutual. Neither would want their daughter to marry one.

And then, in the 'fifties, the new wave: coloured Commonwealth citizens from the West Indies, India and Pakistan.* They inhabit, naturally, the fringes of London and the industrial cities, where unskilled work was then available. Now a generation of British-born coloured children is emerging from education in British schools. Will they be able to take their place in time beside the Celts, or the Huguenots, and become typically British?

I leave it as a question, since there is no answer yet, only a hope. The British are slow to accept 'foreigners' as fellow citizens ... If he was in a rare talkative mood, my father would tell us stories about the men who came into the yard. If they were Jews, as he thought of them in that category, that would be a point of comment. 'Jew-boys', he called them. There was no malice in this, even an affectionate

---

* They came as of right. Citizens of the British Empire had always been led to believe they could claim to be British, as Roman colonists had the right to say, 'Civis Romanus sum,' and could pass as freely between parts of the Empire as, say, between England and Scotland. In 1962, the Immigration Act betrayed that promise. At the moment about one million British inhabitants are coloured. At present rates we can expect, by the year 2000, three or four million in a population of seventy million.

amusement, an appreciation of their exotic style. But none
the less a sense of dealing with foreigners, and therefore
incorrigible rogues: you would be a fool to trust them, but
you got some amusement from the tricks they tried on you.
In his stories they always did the 'right' thing: suddenly
opening a battered suitcase and offering to pay in five-
pound notes; openly appealing to emotion—evidently
counterfeit—mixing tears and personal appeals with the
cold matter of striking a bargain, their gestures as wildly
extravagant as their claims. Some of his first regular cus-
tomers were a Jewish family who came into the yard with a
pony and cart to take away scrap metal from the dump by
the incinerator; they are now reputedly millionaires, with
the traditional trappings, maroon Rolls-Royces, vicuña
coats, villas in Spain. That was a story my father liked to
tell.

And my mother had *her* story that matched that, from
the days when she had been a nurse in a hospital in the
East End. An enormously fat Jewish woman had brought in
her child, who had swallowed a penny. The woman was
wailing and distraught—you would have thought it was the
end of the world. My mother held the child up by its heels
and slapped its back. The penny fell on the floor. That was
the easy part. The trouble was with the child's mother.
She threw herself on my mother, clasping her to her great
breasts, weeping tears of gratitude, calling down God's
blessing on her for saving the life of her child. They could
not get rid of her. Indeed my mother feared for her own
safety, caught in the embrace of this huge, sweating,
blubbering woman ...

'They' were different. That was the simple point of
these tales. 'I think he's one of those,' said with an unob-
trusive nod and a certain meaning expression, twenty years
ago was as likely to mean Jewish as homosexual. Even so,
the real anti-Semitic point of Jewishness had not registered
in my mind. When I went away to boarding school, I was

mystified when one of the masters* said venomously to a
boy in the class, 'I know *your* type. I've taught all through
Golders Green.' Yet I must have realized it was important.
It rattled round my head, unresolved, for years, until I
understood its implications.

That was near the beginning of the war. The horrors of
Hitler's executions have since given us Aryans a sort of
guilt by association. Yet there are residual pockets of anti-
Semitism, no longer overt, but effective still: private schools
that accept only a 'quota' of Jewish children ('We have to
do something,' the lady protested to my objection. 'They're
so *clever*. Our boys would never stand a chance.'); golf
clubs where Jews happen not to be elected; firms where
Jews are not given jobs; families where they are not welcome.

The irony is that we British 'don't trust foreigners', but
we're just a bunch of foreigners ourselves. One can put up a
picture of a true Englishman, and every individual con-
tradicts it. Yet somehow it remains valid. John Bull and
Jack Beaver co-exist—sometimes in the same person. That
is the enigma of the British character. What these two have
in common is their insularity. With perfect arrogance they
can criticize others who have un-English habits. 'If a young
man go to Italy without a prudent tutor,' wrote Roger Ascham in 1570, 'he will fall to popery and filthy living ...
Some Circes shall make him, of a plain Englishman, a
right Italian.'† Ruskin, exquisitely sensitive to the Italian
landscape, liked its people less. 'Take them all in all,' he

---

* A meticulous man, he could bear no more than a couple of terms of us vulgar
boys. I remember him flying into a rage when a boy silently shrugged his shoulders
to indicate he couldn't answer a question. (Could it have been me, imitating a gesture
I had seen at the movies?) The headmaster announced to the whole school, with a
sort of horrified relish, that this man was leaving because he found our manners
appalling and our behaviour at table disgusting.

† At about the same time, Girolamo Cardano—deceived, no doubt, by English
politeness—explained that the English 'dress like the Italians, for they are very
fond of us'. It appeals mightily to the English sense of humour to lead people to
think they are liked when they are not.

said, 'I detest the Italians beyond measure ... Being
essentially unable to talk, they try to make lips of their
fingers. How they poke, wave, flourish, point, shake fingers
and fist ...' D. H. Lawrence, too: 'I loathe and detest the
Italians. They never argue, they just get hold of parrot
phrases, shove up their shoulders and put their heads on
one side and flap their hands ...' Byron loved Italy, but
also rather despised the Italians. However, 'Thou art the
garden of the world,' he wrote. What higher compliment
from an Englishman?

John Bull is brashly patriotic, foxhunting in full rig in
India, bluffly insisting on running up the flag and changing
for dinner in the depths of the jungle. 'According to the
English,' said Stendhal, 'their little island was created to
serve as a model for the universe.' Jack Beaver is *quietly*
patriotic. He is somewhat ashamed of his vulgar relation,
realizing that his bluff insistence on maintaining the English
style, ignoring the native culture, can cover a fear of inadequacy. But he is just as fiercely convinced of English
superiority. At one minute I find myself embarrassed by
jingoism;* at the next, considering, say, police brutality in
Paris, or Texas, relieved that 'it couldn't happen here'.
This is patriotism in another style, and one catches oneself
at it, as one does at superstition—crossing the road just
before you have to decide whether or not to walk under a
ladder.

It is our insularity—the literal fact that we live on an
island—that gives the British their character. John Donne
warned us, recognizing this English tendency: 'No man is
an island.' That concern for privacy, the lace-curtained
windows and the protective hedges round our gardens, our
reluctance to talk to strangers, our pretended lack of interest in the the lives of others: those are the habits of insularity. 'The most hateful of all names in the English ear',

* 'By Jingo!'—a nonsense exclamation, probably like 'By Jove!' a euphemism for
'By God!', was mostly in upper-class usage. Jingoists were aggressively patriotic.

said George Orwell, 'is Nosey Parker.' That famous politeness too, and our lethal charm, are a way of digging a
ditch round ourselves, of keeping people at arm's length.
And that reticence, that deference, the reserve that appears
so often merely to be the fear of appearing ridiculous, that
English understatement, the habits of qualification and
hesitancy and apologetic double-negative in our speech:
they are our manner only, not our nature, a method of
standing off from the thing, allowing ourselves the advantage of non-commitment.

So we find it difficult to be direct. This results in a rare
talent for diplomacy and an unfortunate reputation for
perfidy—saying sorry as we betray our friends. On the
other hand it does give us a sort of gentleness, an abhorrence
of direct violence, a reluctance to offend, a social sentimen-
tality. Arnold Bennett recorded in his journal a story that
typifies the over-sensitive manner of English politeness. A
somewhat unsophisticated foreigner, it seems, was invited
to the house of an English friend. He arrived before the
other guests. The hostess pressed him to take off what
she assumed was his overcoat. He hesitated, but she assured
him one should do so, it was quite the right thing. But to
her consternation, when he took off the coat he revealed
himself in his shirtsleeves. She scarcely knew what to do.
She could not, of course, explain to him her mistake.
Happily the next guest to arrive was a good friend, and an
Englishman. She took him aside and explained her embarrassment. The friend proved to be quick-witted as
well as polite. He himself removed his jacket, and sat for a
minute in his shirtsleeves next to the foreigner; but almost
immediately he complained of the cold, and asked the
hostess if she did not think they might not be more sensible
to resume their jackets, if she did not mind.

The English think of themselves as solid, reliable, honest,
decent folk, not given to folly or silly Continental ways.
They share an island with Scotsmen, one in ten of the

British population, who are 'careful'—that is, mean—and unfriendly,* and the Welsh, one in twenty, who are quick, sing like angels and fight like devils. The Irish, over the water, they drink and talk but they don't like work. There are others: Jews, who are 'different' and suspect; 'darkies', some of whom, surprisingly, seem to have sufficient intelligence to become doctors and civil servants.

To much of the world the typical Englishman is the typical English gentleman: secretive, fair-skinned, masochistic, fey, tweedy, Tory, with that air of quietly expecting to be proved right in the end. For myself I never expect to see a more English sight than a group of Boy Scouts at the 1936 Olympics decorously chanting, in impeccable accents, polite but *keen*, '*We* want you to *win*. *We* want you to *win*.'

Apart from a brother and sister, a mother and father of course, at least one aunt in Brighton and at least two dogs (we had a Sealyham and an Alsatian), the world knows that every Englishman has a nanny. We did not have a nanny, but we did have Ivy.

Ivy was a local woman. Her parents' house was in a turning just along the road from us. She 'lived in' with us, in a small room at the top of the house, and she and my mother shared the work between them. I do not recall that she wore a uniform; she was fond of clothes in a colour she called 'wine', but I think that was a personal taste. She was a big, slow-moving woman who laughed little, a great churchgoer, with the secretive self-righteousness that sometimes goes with that habit. She was often moody, and silently resentful, refusing to explain her grievances, until her mother would have to come round and set it right. She ate her meals apart from us, in the kitchen. She had that national weakness, a sweet tooth: in the war she kept her

---

* In a hotel just over the border in Scotland I commented to the receptionist (naturally) on the weather. 'You had the best summer of the whole country,' I said. 'Och no,' she said firmly. 'The whole of *Scotland* has had a good summer.' Less than three hundred years ago, after all, it was a foreign country.

jam ration—a pound a month, I believe—separately from ours, and my mother often gave her another jar from her own making; but she could never make it last until more was due.

There was a bell behind the door in the dining-room (installed, I imagine, before my parents moved in), and at the end of each course we children would ask, 'Can I ring the bell?' Ivy would bring the next course and clear away the dishes. In time this system was discarded and the bell fell into disuse. We would take out the dishes ourselves, 'to save Ivy', or would take her pudding down the hall to her instead of the quick ring that told her she should come to fetch it. But she still ate alone in the kitchen.

I am not aware of feeling much affection for Ivy. She was merely there. But she considered us 'her' children—particularly the youngest, my sister. She was outraged one day when taking us for a walk to be stopped by a woman who asked, Did she get her little girl's hair so curly with 'Shirley Temple' shampoo? She took us for a walk most afternoons, respectable with clean gloves and bonnets and leggings with long rows of buttons. We liked to walk through the farmyard and, on Tuesdays, through the cattle market. But Ivy liked most of all to watch weddings at the church. My mother did not like us to wait outside with the local old ladies, but Ivy never missed a wedding if she could help. On her day off we would see her hurrying 'up the town' to make sure she did not miss seeing the bride come out.

Ivy's father worked in the Mills. The Mills were to us what a pit would be to a mining town. It was the largest local employer, mysterious and dangerous. The men were searched as they went in to make sure they did not have matches on them. There were occasional accidents. Ivy's father narrowly escaped with his life after one explosion: his clothes were on fire, but he ran to the river and threw himself in. We children went once or twice with Ivy to his house to see his canaries, flying in an aviary in the little back garden. The first time I ever went into a pub was to see some of his birds in a competition held in the saloon bar of a local pub. Outside, pubs seemed such mysterious places. It was a surprise to find an ordinary interior.

2. *Queen Elizabeth Sleeps Here*

I do love these ancient ruins.
We never tread upon them but we set
Our foot upon some reverend history.
> John Webster, *The Duchess of Malfi* (1614)

Where'er I wander, boast of this I can
Though banished yet a true-born Englishman.
> William Shakespeare, *Richard II* (1595–6)

What is called monarchy appears to me a silly, contemptible thing. I compare it to something kept behind a curtain, about which there is a great deal of bustle and fuss, and a wonderful air of seeming solemnity; but when, by any accident, the curtain happens to open, and the company see what it is, they burst into laughter.
> Tom Paine (1737–1809)

If you once permit the ignorant class to begin to rule, you may bid farewell to deference for ever.
> Walter Bagehot (1826–77)

According to the modern custom, my father's body was cremated. Later his ashes were buried among the old gravestones of the churchyard under a small, simple stone, sunk a couple of inches to allow the mower to pass over. Moss has filled in the letters of his name. Fifty yards away is the grave of King Harold, shot in the eye by an arrow at the Battle of Hastings.* Almost a thousand years separate them.

It is these juxtapositions that make history real. The stones survive. Ancient houses, castles, palaces, occur throughout Britain. 'Queen Elizabeth Slept Here' is a joke —though Elizabeth was a remarkably mobile queen, cannily reducing the cost of maintaining her court by making 'progress' round the great houses of her subjects— but what it expresses is an important sense of history. Even if Elizabeth did not sleep here, she might have done.

And it is, significantly, Elizabeth and not any other monarch whose name is thus taken in vain. We look back to Tudor times as the great and glorious age of our history. 'Young, light-hearted England', G. M. Trevelyan describes it under Elizabeth. A mere four million Englishmen (we are $55\frac{1}{2}$ million now) inhabited what seems to us to have been a sort of paradise. Visitors commented on the richness of the crops, the abundance of meat, the vast flocks of sheep that grazed on the uplands. Even here God smiled:

* 1066: one of the three dates that every Englishman knows (the others are Magna Carta and the Fire of London: 'Sixteen sixty-six, the Fire of London burnt like sticks'). The usual punishment when I was at school was to be given 'dates'. 'Ten times dates' meant having to write out ten times, on specially ruled paper — which had to be bought for a penny or so — a set of about twenty dates, with sentences describing their importance. I must have written them thousands of times, but I cannot recall one of them now.

the undernourished sheep on those thin pastures produced wool of a better quality than their fat lowland kind. And wool was making England rich. Nature was bountiful. 'England,' wrote Fynes Moryson in 1617, 'yea, perhaps one county thereof, hath more fallow deer than all Europe that I have seen. No kingdom in the world hath so many dove houses.' Deer poaching was a national pastime. Hares and bustards (now extinct in western Europe) were hunted across the open land. Townsmen were still in contact with the country. Even London, with a population of two hundred thousand soon to be the largest city in Europe, was still mostly contained within the city walls; and even in that area, the Bishop of Ely's house, for instance, in Holborn, was famous for its fruit gardens. Sheep were grazing in Kensington and the milk came in from the farms of Chelsea.

A new gentry of merchants, lawyers, yeoman farmers, were replacing the old nobility. The undoubted crudity of life was refined by the flowering of the English Renaissance, but still preserved a robust and earthy vigour. Shakespeare was the incarnation of this spirit. Poetry was in fashion. The music at court rivalled any in Europe. At last—it seems now—the English were able to throw off the domination of the Pope and the Church of Rome, free to follow their own nature. From contemporary portraits those Elizabethans, dressed in their impressive finery, look out with a certain sharp confidence, a contained impatience that indicates they consider they have better things to do than sit for a likeness.

The energy of these men looked beyond England for satisfaction; the Elizabethans were great traders, a nation of shipkeepers. The Merchant Adventurers wrested the trade of northern Europe from the Germans. Charters were granted for trade in Muscovy, the Baltic, the Levant, the Indies. The charter of the East India Company was granted in 1600; from that eventually an Indian empire grew. In

Africa, they began by trading and continued with slaving. The flag followed trade. They colonized Virginia. In the Arctic the first whaling ships began to operate.

In the seas again, Nature seemed to be on England's side. Cod was plentiful in the waters of Newfoundland, discovered by John Cabot in 1497. Even habitats changed, to the benefit of the English: 'Herrings,' wrote William Camden, in *Britannia*, in 1586, 'which in the times of our grandfathers swarmed only about Norway, now in our times by the bounty of Providence swim in great shoals round our coasts every year.' Coal, iron, lead, copper, tin were extensively mined. You can understand the enviable confidence of those privileged Elizabethans: such iron 'appeareth to be a particular blessing of God given only to England, for the defence thereof, for albeit most countries have their iron, yet none of them all have iron of that toughness and validity to make such ordnance of'. Even below ground God was on their side. How could the Armada hope to challenge that?

This is the myth of a carefree, maytime country, the false memory of youth that Britain, now ageing, recalls fondly but inaccurately. At a distance murder, plunder and heartless self-interest seem like youthful high spirits. They merge with memories of our own childhood, the vision of life as 'one long picnic'. Certain places retain this association: village greens, country houses, flower gardens; the nostalgia of Anne Hathaway's cottage, in which personal fantasy is confused with national history; 'coaching scene' Christmas cards; the British Travel Association version of Britain (hinting that Shakespeare is still alive); stockbroker's Tudor (William Cobbett had another name for it: 'tax-eater's showy') – all make a point from maytime connections.

None of us is free from the Elizabethan nostalgia. For me it acts most powerfully in Cambridge. For one thing the links are so visibly direct. An Elizabethan map of the

University is perfectly familiar: the same streets are marked — Trumpington Street and Petty Cury; the college buildings laid out as they are now. The city has a maytime atmosphere. Cows graze within sight of King's College chapel, punts slide in among the colleges laden with the scent of the Granchester meadows, and on Mayday itself madrigals are sung on Magdalene tower. May Week, indeed, and the May balls, are the Cambridge tradition almost best known to the outside world.

A perfect physical representation of that maytime spirit of robust elegance stands in the college I went to, Caius (pronounced 'keys'). Dr Caius, who refounded Gonville Hall as Gonville and Caius College in 1557, planned three gates in the 'modern' style (he was much influenced by Continental travel) — of Humility, Virtue and Honour, the last leading directly to the Senate House, where honours are conferred. Only the Gate of Honour was ever built. As it was originally (it was not long ago restored to something like that splendour) it was a solid stone gateway, elaborately decorated with Renaissance classical detail, touched up with gilding and coloured paint — beautiful, vigorous and uninhibited. That's exactly how we see those charmed Elizabethan Englishmen.

The random memories of my own childhood too often throw up mythical golden days. Our house had been the doctor's house that stood next to my father's workshop. It was a substantial building, large enough for two families to live quite separately, with three entrances, a front hall and a back hall and eight rooms on the ground floor. In the war, after Uncle Tom and Auntie Lil had gone off to grow tomatoes, we had army officers billeted on us. One of my maytime memories is of the beautiful blonde lady rocking lazily on the swing that hung from the mulberry tree on the lawn. She was the visiting wife of one of our officers — Mrs Armstrong-Jones.

While Uncle Tom and Auntie Lil were still there, Uncle

Bill—being my father's uncle, actually my great-uncle—used to spend Sunday with each family in turn. He lived about a mile away and he would come by bus every week in time for lunch, dressed winter and summer in his Sunday suit, with the gold watch-chain looped across his round barrel belly. I do not know how they entertained him next door, but with us the routine was almost always the same. In summer he would sit in a deckchair down by the river while we children fished (my brother was a serious fisherman; I preferred to catch minnows or small perch among the tree-roots close to the bank, where I could watch the fish come to the bait). In winter he would sit for a couple of hours by the fire after lunch, and then, after tea, we would persist until he agreed to play Beat-your-neighbour-out-of-doors. For some reason it was never as exciting when we tried playing with anyone else. After my uncle and aunt moved away, Uncle Bill still only came to us every other Sunday. My parents asked him out of a sense of duty, and it was probably very boring for them. He also had habits which we children were beginning to laugh at surreptitiously. His tea, for instance, he tipped into his saucer and supped rather noisily through his moustache. I suppose he did not even hold his knife properly, and we were beginning to learn these sophisticated things—like how you never *cut* your toast at breakfast, you *tear* it, that sort of thing. What my parents never knew, I am sure, was that down there on the old seat in the orchard, or under the chestnuts by the river bank, Uncle Bill used sometimes to ask my brother and me to undo our trousers so that he could see that we were growing up properly. Fortunately he seemed satisfied that we were.

Halfway up the stairs of the house was a window-ledge, three or four feet deep, where I would sit and look out into the garden. Round the edge of the window was a border of small panes of coloured glass. If you looked through the yellow, green was intensified and the grass and trees were rich emerald. Through the blue, it was an underwater world. And the red cast a sinister darkness over it all, with deep shadows and black flowers. I dreamed there for hours, transforming the garden into different worlds. The lawn was marked out as a tennis court, with the old mulberry tree to one side; there were foot-high box hedges enclosing the vegetable plots; asparagus beds; victoria plums growing against the walls; and apples, pears, greengages, damsons in the orchard ...

Now even the house is demolished. And my memories are of rare, untypical occasions. Halcyon days—there *were* kingfishers nesting at the bottom of the garden. In fact they were strange, probably lonely times. We had acquired the furniture of gracious living—the tennis court, private fishing, Ivy in the kitchen waiting for the bell, Barnard tending the asparagus beds—but we did not know how to use it. My mother had hopeful visions of weekend visitors, tennis parties of eligible young people. But they did not happen.

It might seem absurd to see in a few tiny accidents (Mrs Armstrong-Jones, stepmother-in-law of the Queen's sister; the proximity of King Harold's tomb; the fallow deer in Epping Forest near by*) links with royalty, but these tenuous connections are important. The British have an emotional commitment to royalty. Did they not sing, just before my time, my brother's friends, 'Hark the herald angels sing, Mrs Simpson stole our King'? While we have a royal family we have a direct contact with those fairy-tale times. Every Englishman who dreams has at one time or another encountered the Royal Family, imposing themselves surreally on our domestic scene: Princess Margaret at table, impatiently waiting for you to finish with the salt; Prince Philip mysteriously substituting himself for your

* These deer, protected for Henry VIII to hunt, have evolved in the sunless forest into a distinct variety, dark and spotless. At night occasionally a hundred green eyes would reflect our headlights beside the road. My brother ran into one once and broke its leg. He had to slit its throat and drag it into the ditch.

uncle in a game of french cricket. 'I find', said Dr Johnson, after a conversation with George III, 'it does a man good to be talked to by his sovereign.' Most of us do not expect an actual encounter, but we are none the less quite prepared for one. We shall never need them, but we know the rules of royal conversation: never speak until spoken to, and address Her Majesty as 'Ma'am' (pronounced 'marm'). And if it comes to a meal, I am not at all sure that Her Majesty might not be allergic to shellfish.

We never come across the Prime Minister in our sleep, because his is the unpopular practical function of government. It is by not governing that the monarchy has retained its status. The British will even tolerate a woman in the job, since they know she will have male advisers who will ensure she makes no mistakes.* Yet actually Britain was never more powerful than under her two great queens, Elizabeth and Victoria.

When I was fifteen I would stand properly to attention when they played the National Anthem in the cinema. I believe I often sang the words. Certainly if we went to the theatre we sang: my father in a low, tuneless growl; my mother somewhat delicately; my sister, who had a good voice, rather loud. Now it's a rare royalist who hesitates to leave while the Anthem is playing. Yet I do remember, when George VI died, and I was in the Army, the professional soldiers were affected. For them it was a personal loss: they held the King's commission. For me, as a conscript, I experienced the ceremonies of memorial and dedication—'The King is Dead, Long Live the Queen'—with the sense merely of history. This was the moment when Elizabeth II was added to that long list of Henrys, Edwards and Georges in the reference books.

Monarchy survives by adaptation, taking its role from

---

* Twenty-one per cent of adults in a representative poll in 1970 declared that, if we had to have a 'dictator', the Duke of Edinburgh would be the best man. The Queen was backed by only 4 per cent. Significantly, Enoch Powell ran the Duke a close second.

the requirements of its subjects and its tone from the style of the time. The signature of Magna Carta, even the somewhat forced humility of its tone, was the admission that monarchy was a doomed institution. 'To no one will we sell, to no one deny or delay right or justice.' That is our guarantee of freedom, and we none of us forget it. Those are the terms on which we have tolerated monarchy. A failure to understand the nature of this bargain lost Charles I his head; others have needed tactful but firm reminders.* Our nature requires a compromise course. We are killing off the monarchy slowly, administering accumulating doses of disrespect, a thousand-year course of poison. We rejected the crude methods of the Rump Parliament, when they declared that 'the Commons in England have supreme power in this nation' and executed the king: that is not the English manner. Recoiling in horror from what we had done, we restored Charles II and continued our solicitous administration. Now the monarchy is a thin, ailing thing, not much more than a real-life TV serial. Everyone will admit that the Queen 'does a wonderful job'. They all do, the entire Royal Family, showing themselves wherever they are persuaded it might be useful, flashing smiles and jewellery, imperturbably radiant.

Ironically, the last serious role the monarchy plays is a protection for the democratic constitution. By being informed of the routine working of government business (the boxes of state papers that follow the Queen wherever she travels) the monarch keeps open an eye jealous for constitutional irregularities. And at times of crisis—the death of a Prime Minister in office, the repeated defeat of a govern-

---

* Edward II, for instance, whose lordly contempt for his subjects finally lost him, too, his throne and his life. At the parliament meeting at Stamford in 1309, it was put to him, in charming medieval franglais (the Puritans later referred sharply to 'brackish French', but it is worth taking the trouble to puzzle out, for the sound of it): 'Les bones gentz du roialme qi sont cy venuz au parlement prient a nostre seyneur le roi qil voille, si lui plest, aver regard de son povre people, qe molt se sent grave, de ceo qil ne sont pas menez si come il deussent estre, nommement des pointz de la Grand Chartre, e prie de ce, si lui plest, remedie.'

ment with a small majority, a coalition – action is required. True, it would be possible to arrange for this duty to be carried out by other bodies, but as we are at present constituted, it is the function of the Crown.

I myself could wish to see the Royal Family more apparently stimulated by their opportunity. They could attract the best brains in every field – historians, philosophers, scientists: almost no one would refuse their invitation. Their table, their holidays, their interminable travelling, could be enlivened by the most brilliant men in the country. We need the intellectual stimulus of a monarch evidently possessing a good mind, and using it.* At present the Royal Family give evidence of merely middle-class manners, polite English expressions of interest, modernized by a certain calculated breeziness. The children would be a credit to any middle-class family: they seem energetic, tidy, confident, and quite straight, with an easy manner and a cheerful respect for their parents. But perhaps this is the more sophisticated way: most people aspire to a middle-class life, and this is the fairy-tale version.

Certainly it was to this royal version of middle-class life that my family and their friends aspired. Politically they were Puritan conservatives, a cruel – but in some ways innocent – persuasion, based on the sanctity of work. Like everyone else, their way of life was threatened by 'them'. Their conservatism was one method of protecting possessions. The crime of 'them', who broadly speaking consisted of the left-minded – socialists, the Labour Party, the Co-op, the unions (probably Communist inspired), liberal intellectuals – was to encourage men to expect reward without work, to take more out of the social kitty than the value of what they put in. My

* In those golden days of Elizabeth I, the Queen was an intellectual too. Roger Ascham, once her tutor, was proud of his pupil: 'Yea, I believe that beside her perfit readiness in Latin, Italian, French and Spanish she readeth here at Windsor more Greek every day, than some Prebendaries of this Church doth read Latin in a whole weeke.'

father paid his men higher than the union rate, but he would not employ union men. I do not doubt that he was a fair, even a good employer. He himself had achieved prosperity by simple and unflagging hard work. He started with no more privilege than any of the men who worked for him, and I should have expected some sympathy for them. But his whole life was sacrificed to work, and those who expected something more were under suspicion of idleness. When he died, my father left a large estate, but he never lived like a rich man. He would not take money out of the firm he had built up. One of his few luxuries was expensive cigarettes. He never smoked in the house, only in the yard. In the drawer of his desk there was always a box of Player's *Perfectos*. 'Have a Woodbine, boy,' he would say as he offered you one.

In their youth my parents and most of their friends had known difficult times. They came from homes where the money had to be watched. They had lived through the Depression, and that had filled them with a sort of satisfying fear. My father's first job was in a pawnshop, an experience from which anyone might develop a fear of credit — but in fact this attitude was common to all his friends. It was the very fact of surmounting difficult times that gives this Puritan conservatism a suspicious turn. The work-worship is perverted into a sort of persecution. There is guilt present also, at having survived successfully when others have not — to be assuaged by continued work and the self-pretence of not enjoying the benefits of money. What these people fear is not the simple moral possibility that the idle might be undeservedly rewarded, but that the idle might be rewarded from profits that might otherwise have been theirs. They are mocked by the vision of that mythical labourer, father of six, who does not bother to find work, since social security pays him as well. With no better outlet for his energy, he simply begets more children. Idling and copulating at their expense: that is naturally galling. So socialism seems to be a plot to take money from those who have justly earned it and squander it on layabouts.

Over thirty years our family had three sets of friends. Others came and went, but these were permanent: the Wattses, the Haylocks and the Sweetenhams. For us they took the place of relatives, to whom we made only rather formal visits. None of these friends lived in the same town as us, but they were all within ten or fifteen miles. The Haylocks and the Wattses were originally business acquaintances. Mr Watts ran a small hire-purchase finance business. Mr Haylock, an engineering works where he could regrind valves or make up the special parts my father sometimes needed (new spare parts were hard to come by in the war). The Sweetenhams had been met on holiday. Mr Sweetenham had been a professional soldier, and he had not lost the manner – children did not climb on his lap. And the Wattses were as socially nervous as us, which created a certain tension. It was only with the Haylocks that we were really at home. We were weekly visitors to each other's houses, and their two children were like brother and sister to us. Only with them were we confident enough to risk the final intimacy of going on holiday together. Yet I never learnt to call either of them anything less formal than Mr and Mrs.

Whereas there was always the possibility that relatives — Uncle Bill, say — might be inclined to vote for 'them', my parents and their friends were loyal Conservative voters. Not that they were politically active; there were no political discussions round our tea table. Party loyalty had difficult class associations, and was embarrassing to talk about. And politics was anyway a suspect profession, and politicians under suspicion of preferring talk to honest work. But my mother would turn out on election day to drive disabled Conservative voters to the polls: it was commonly assumed that we were all Conservative.

For some years my father was chairman of the local Conservative Association. But this was a social, not a political position. He was not a man to make a speech. Indeed, he rarely attended meetings, and my mother had the greatest difficulty in getting him to the annual dance at any sort of reasonable time. (But it was the same whenever we went out: he never came in from the yard early enough to have time to get ready—each of us would go down in turn, ready washed and changed, to 'see if he was coming'. The more we chivvied him, the longer he took. He was a stubborn man.) But for the local Conservatives participation was not necessary. Simply, as the owner of one of the largest businesses in the neighbourhood, he took the title as a natural duty. The Association amounted to a local trade-protection society.

Our suburban community was self-reliant. Though only fifteen miles away, London was like the local market town that happened to be the capital. You went there to buy clothes, and occasionally for a night out. Only young people, the girls and boys who were typists and clerks, went daily to offices in the city. We were not a dormitory suburb. The leaders of the community were local men—the doctor,* the bank manager, the vicar, a solicitor, successful builders and shopkeepers. Mr Scott, the baker, and Mary, his daughter, who rather gave herself county airs (the voice, the charm spread all over like butter-icing), were active leaders of the Conservative Association.

Around Christmas, these people, and the various friends, would be asked to 'a little cocktail party'. Relatives never came to these functions. The Haylocks often ducked them too. They were nervous occasions. Great trouble was taken with plates of delicate smoked-salmon sandwiches in Hovis,

---

* There was no dentist. We travelled a couple of miles for this regular torture (this was before the days of high-speed drills), to the surgery of Mr Douglas, an Australian who practised on the ground floor of an ordinary semi-detached house. Over twenty years he had a succession of young Australian partners—and I still have the idea that Australia must be full of ambitious young dentists with scrubbed fingernails.

and hot *miniature* sausage-rolls. Too many flower arrange-
ments were put about—and much commented on by the
ladies. We children were called upon to display the gentlemanly manners and the accent we were so expensively
acquiring. 'Well now,' Mr Watts would say, or 'Uncle
Harry', the husband of one of my mother's nursing friends,
'—Well, now,' they would say, with a forced joviality,
kindly but with an ominous tone, 'have you made up your
mind yet what you're going to do ?' At fourteen, not to have
a career planned was made to seem distinctly frivolous.

But if I did not have a career mapped out, I had already
blindly absorbed a nervous social aspiration. Without
explicit ambition, it admitted established aims, established
ways. You question values when it is open to you to accept
or reject the status that maintains them. Criticism is not
open to aspirants. Getting a good school report, becoming
a prefect or head of house, getting a commission in the
Army: there was no doubt that for me these were creditable
achievements. They were somehow to be the product of
my father's own hard work and leisureless toil. The Puritan
doctrine of deferred reward, slightly displaced: our achievements would be his reward. He never realized, nor for
many years did I, that, in a certain sense, hard work is easy.
Virtuous in itself, it disbars the dangerous possibilities of
choice, and imagination, and disconcerting questions. Hard
work leaves no time for philosophy.

Stanley Baldwin, three times Conservative Prime
Minister in the 'twenties and 'thirties, had a reputation for
cultivated indolence. He was the real pipe-smoking super-
relaxed English type, to whom it appears to come as such a
surprise when things go wrong—equally when they go right.
'Whichever party may be in office,' Baldwin confidently
claimed, 'the Conservatives are always in power.'

Though the Honourable Hugh Adeane Vivian Smith
is a reticent, mild-mannered man, his appointment

as chairman of Charter Consolidated in the steps of Harry Oppenheimer himself is not such a surprise. He is, of course, one of the formidable family of financial Smiths.

Mr Smith has been with Anglo American on and off since 1945. He was invited to go and work for the group just after the war, from which he emerged as a major in the Irish Guards with a military M.B.E. ...

His main strength in the group is on the financial side. Married to Lady Helen Primrose, Hugh Smith is the uncle of the present Lord Bicester, and is very well connected in the City.

This from a recent *Times*. Who can doubt that Stanley Baldwin is still correct, and that the Chairman of Charter Consolidated can be relied on to vote for the Conservative Party? The Conservatives are always in power because the men of influence in the City (bankers and stockbrokers), the powerful industrialists, much of the civil service, the Church, and what used quaintly to be called 'the professions' (the law, teachers in private schools, professional service officers, medicine, perhaps accountancy and certain types of farming) are predominantly Conservative. And years of indoctrination have instilled in many others a habit of absent-minded deference. One third of the working class (if that is still a definable category) vote Conservative. 'The Tory people are the brains of the country,' they say. 'They know how to get things done.' Partly this deference is laziness. Partly it acts out the two central British characteristics: the desire not to get involved and sturdy self-confidence. Political influence, in the wide sense, is easily available, but few Englishmen make use of it. They do not *expect* to have their opinions acted on. The small, hard core of the vocal middle class is always showing the way, diverting motorways, preserving Georgian terraces, moving airports ... they can work miracles, literally moving mountains. But the rest remain silent. They doubt their political competence. So the establishment continues to rule.

And however we imagine we despise them, most of us are impressed by titles and honours. Honours are traditionally bestowed for favours rendered, and the greater honours have always in one way or another been directly purchasable. Lloyd George's tariff is well known: ten thousand pounds for a knighthood, thirty thousand pounds for a baronetcy, fifty to one hundred thousand for a peerage. Today discreet charity is still effective (don't forget to take into account fifty years' inflation), and real achievement is also recognized. Blindly anachronistic, the Queen celebrates her birthday* by issuing an honours list dictated by the Prime Minister.

What function does the peerage now perform? Like the stars of old Hollywood, peers seem unable to adapt to a role that makes sense in modern society. The House of Lords has a thousand members, and three hundred and thirty-three is the largest attendance in the last twenty-five years. Yet when in 1967 the Queen's Speech promised that the next session of parliament would 'reduce the power of the House of Lords and eliminate its hereditary bias', there was deafening protest. *Democracy*, it seemed, was being interfered with.

Nor is it in the British tradition to reform the constitution by statute. We have no written constitution. The mother of parliaments has herself no birth certificate — and we are proud of the fact. So it seems that the House of Lords, reformed without legislation, will fossilize itself into a lifeless monument to human vanity. There is no need to take dramatic measures. The peerage will die slowly, delivering the grand country houses to the National Trust, or to the new leisure industry, at a rate at which they can be absorbed,

---

* This is her official birthday, in June, which serves as an excuse for the swankiest military parades of the year. With our climate these as often suffer bad weather as her actual birthday, April 21st.

to be enjoyed for what they now are—part of the national inheritance.

Yet we continue to be impressed. Why else should dedicated socialists allow themselves to be addressed, 'Lord', 'Baroness', to parade in cloaks trimmed with ermine? To take as an *honour* the Order of the British Empire—can that be innocent of vanity, or snobbery? And the rest of us encourage it. We may disagree, but we *are* impressed. The saying is true: 'We all love a lord.' It would be false to claim that I can talk to a lord, or even a knight, without rank intruding between us. I have been indoctrinated with habits of deference. In my case deference was due to status as well as class: even doctors and teachers could expect it. When I was about fourteen I was taken to a nasal specialist on account of some small defect. He was a kindly, white-haired man. Not very special. But first thing as we came out of his rooms my mother said to me, in a shocked tone—obviously it had embarrassed her during the whole interview—'Why didn't you call him "Sir"?'

In fact politics gives fewer and fewer opportunities for the brilliant individual. Government has become responsible democracy. We are ruled not by 'statesmen' but by departments of the civil service, given spurious modernity with zingy new names. No longer a Ministry of Labour. No Postmaster General. No simple Ministry of Education, or of Health. Instead, positive, modern titles: Minister of Employment and *Productivity*; Minister of Posts and *Telecommunications*; of Education and *Science*; of Health and *Social Security*. We have a Ministry of Technology, further modernized by its own abbreviation, MinTech. We have a Department of the Environment. But behind the flashy names there is less scope for the political career-ist, hoping for glamour and useful connections. Parliament itself, after its Victorian zenith, grows feeble. Its debates are spineless, the tone often so shamefully infantile that the refusal to allow TV cameras into the chamber appears like a deliberate and necessary act of self-preservation. * Yet the establishment, perpetuating itself, is able to look on government as a more or less irritating necessity. A Labour government, naturally, is less welcome to, and itself touchy towards, such institutions as the City and the Law. The aloof, intractable B.B.C. pleases neither party.†

'The British people,' Disraeli said, with a sort of mad logic, 'being subject to fogs, and possessing a powerful middle class, require great statesmen.' Now we are all middle class; and we have eliminated those Victorian pea-soupers with the Clean Air Act, which has reduced London smoke by 60 per cent. Now we could not stomach great statesmen, unless they disguise themselves as ordinary men. Even a Conservative Prime Minister is better not of the establishment but created as its servant. Edward Heath, for instance, seems to have been chosen deliberately to refute accusations of privilege: here is a leader, socially gauche, his vowel-sounds ineradicably common, the very model of a modern bureaucrat. He, or someone like him, will serve perfectly well.

Once, though, we were ruled by our heroes. You can

---

* 'Sir Walter Bromley-Davenport (Conservative, Knutsford), who appeared to be deeply shocked by Mr Lubbock's language, had earlier told Mr David Winnick (Labour, Croydon S.) to "shove your dentures back in your kisser".' (Parliamentary report in the *Guardian*, 1970).

† Established by royal charter, and not by parliament (as was commercial television), with true British duality, the B.B.C. is considered by many the archetype of the establishment, yet it has fiercely guarded its independence. Lord Reith, its founder, declared that 'the broadcasting system of a nation is a mirror of that nation's conscience.' 'Our only obligation', added Sir William Haley, a later Director-General, 'is to do the right thing.' A Labour government will always be convinced that this B.B.C. right thing is the Conservative thing. Certainly the B.B.C. has always supported established ways. (In the 'thirties the newsreaders had to wear dinner-jackets even for the radio bulletins.) Yet, equally, Conservative Prime Ministers have accused the B.B.C. of bias against them, and it is a common Conservative criticism that the B.B.C. is staffed with left-wing intellectual pansies. As that indicates, the B.B.C. does compromise magnificently. Unfortunately, compromise is not always the best way to the truth. Timidity on the part of the B.B.C., E. M. Forster pointed out forty years ago, will not stop it being influential, and that influence will 'confirm thousands in our congenital habit of avoiding unwelcome truth'.

judge a nation, as you can a man, by its heroes. Henry VIII, Elizabeth I, Drake, Raleigh, Nelson, Wellington, Churchill: these have been the British heroes. And behind them a string of semi-legendary figures: Boadicea, King Arthur, King Alfred, Lady Godiva, King Harold, Richard the Lion-Heart, Robert the Bruce, Dick Whittington, Robin Hood, Shakespeare, Dr Johnson, Queen Victoria—these inhabit the shadowy land where history becomes myth. Is it King Arthur himself or *Camelot* we remember, susceptible now to the influence of influence?

Our heroes were a strange set. Some qualities you would expect from all heroes: vitality, a certain arrogance, luck, courage, hypocrisy, patriotism. But is such a keen regard for appearances essential? Drake was hugely vain, Churchill abnormally aware of the opinion of others (in 1897 he wrote to his mother from India, 'I rode on my grey pony all along the skirmish line where everyone else was lying down in cover. Foolish perhaps, but I play for high stakes and given an audience there is no act too daring or too noble. Without the gallery things are very different.'); Nelson was a great publicity seeker and, according to Wellington, 'vain and silly'. And that tendency to childishness is common too: Henry VIII, when crossed, sulked like a petulant boy; Churchill was boyish and impulsive. Most of our heroes suffered fits of depression. All but Wellington had naval connections: Henry VIII is known as the 'father of the British navy'—so are others, including King Alfred and Samuel Pepys; Churchill was First Lord of the Admiralty at the outbreak of World War II, and throughout his life he continued to emphasize his honorary title of Warden of the Cinque Ports.*

Few of our heroes are the giants of legend. Bluff King Hal was a big man, and Wellington was of average height. But Drake was known as 'the little captain'; Nelson was a

---

* These are the five ports nominated by Henry VIII to provide his navy. The pronunciation is quite anglicized, in the medieval manner: 'sink' ports.

tiny man — five foot two or three inches; Churchill was very
short, with a chest measurement, when he entered Sandhurst, of thirty-one inches.

Wellington is perhaps a doubtful British hero. His
achievements were heroic enough, but as a person he was
too like the rest of us, too English for the English to love.
And too cold. 'I like to walk alone,' he simply explained.
We do not feel warmth for him as we do for the roguish
Drake, fiery Elizabeth, insufferable Henry. We prefer
naughty heroes. And Wellington was modest ('I believe',
he wrote to his brother, 'that I have been on the whole the
most fortunate and most favoured of God's creatures, and
if I don't forget the above-mentioned, I think I may yet do
well'), with a great sense of service and duty. He was fair
but strict, the 'Iron Duke' with a soft heart, who wept to
see his men, by his own order, hanged to deter others from
rape and plunder. He was no reformer: he objected to the
growth of the railways because, he said, 'they would encourage the lower classes to move about.' After twelve years
abroad he returned faithfully to marry Kitty Pakenham,
the girl to whom he had promised that he would not change
his mind. She seemed a different person. 'She has grown
ugly, by Jove,' he said to his brother. But he married her
none the less; he had given his word. You cannot get more
English than that.

We have no need for heroes now. Winston Churchill,
A. J. P. Taylor has said, 'incorporated the resolve of the
British people at what was probably the last great moment
of their history'. That moment passed before I was ten.
Educated for twentieth, or at least late-nineteenth, century
society, the heroes I was encouraged to admire were much
more the Boy Scout type. What we learnt of the heroes of
history seemed like mere adventure stories. 'At Flores
in the Azores Sir Richard Grenville lay ... ' 'Into the valley
of death rode the Six Hundred ...' These colourful characters, somehow all Tudor contemporaries, inhabited the

same country as Robin Hood and the Sheriff of Nottingham: round the coasts, Francis Drake, having at the last moment abandoned his game of bowls, cheekily dismissed the Barbary pirates, who were also Spanish infidels; overland the Dragoon Guards, with pike and musket, defended Europe from Napoleon and the Boche.

These were imaginary figures. Our real heroes were those who could claim harmless, quasi-military achievements — climbing Everest, or crossing Antarctica. I never understood why it was considered creditable to do these uncomfortable things. Why sail alone round the world? Because it is there? After a recent global yacht race, Robin Knox-Johnston recalled that 'to some extent I got going because I knew there was a very strong French challenger and I thought, I'm darned if the French are going to beat me. Then, while I was coming up the Atlantic I heard on my radio receiver that de Gaulle had insulted our ambassador, Christopher Soames. I thought, what bloody impertinence, and went and put up more sail. I wrote in my log: "De Gaulle has given me an extra six miles today." ' 'I do not regret this journey,' Scott wrote in his diary, knowing he was soon to die in the blizzard, 'which has shown that Englishmen can endure hardship, help one another, and meet death with as great a fortitude as ever in the past.' I am bewildered by this jingoism.

The 'quasi-military' lesson that we were expected to learn at school was that of *leadership*. In his report for my last term at prep school, this was the only aspect of my personality that the headmaster commented on: 'Has powers of leadership.' Our hero would be head of a team, equal but superior, ready — eager even — to suffer frostbite with his men, cheering them through difficulties, strict but fair. It is the British habit of superficial morality. Eminence within the system is desirable; to question the system itself is bad form. Let us deplore the 'irreconcilable wrongness of war'. But let us never question our country if it chooses to wage one. The hero we were set to worship was the servant of society, efficient and selfless, Jack Beaver, with his great English quality of *reliability*. But our hero had another characteristic—leadership. And the sacrifice of self was ennobled by a vaguely religious sense of communion with God through Nature—muscular mysticism, with only soft questions asked and woolly answers given.

'Irreconcilable wrongness' is a phrase of George Mallory, himself a fine example of the muscular mystic. He fought in World War I with a sense of almost religious duty. The perfect *imago* of this hero type, a scholar in mathematics at King's College, Cambridge, in that weird pre-war period when the University hothouse nourished such orchids as Keynes, Lytton Strachey, Rupert Brooke, Duncan Grant, John Sheppard.* Mallory was serious, civilized, with the astonishing and moving depth of integrity found in the perfect specimen. His beauty was celebrated (the body by Praxiteles, the Botticelli face—that was Strachey's infatuated view), but he despised concern with such superficial matters. Instead he exercised his physical gifts in mountaineering. He 'climbed with miraculous grace and ease'. His approach was practical and prudent, but his inspiration was exceedingly lofty. Climbing was like listening to the greatest music, the adventure without which he would run the risk of 'drying up like a pea in its shell'. In 1924, making for the summit of Everest, 'going strong for the top', that 'unimaginable English boy' (Strachey again) disappeared into the mists at twenty-eight thousand feet. His own shining goodness, that quality so difficult to appreciate from a distance, and the mystic implications of that end (blending the two great British influences—a sort of Christian Assumption from Olympus) made him the hero of his generation.

My education would have made Mallorys of us all.

---

* Classical scholar and translator of Greek tragedies. In the 1950s, when I was at Cambridge, Sir John still shuffled about the Great Court of King's, an object of slight curiosity to us callow undergraduates.

Indeed, with more or less success, it has. And I feel I know Mallory's qualities, because I knew at school a boy who could have taken his place without even Strachey noticing the difference. The boy I knew never achieved fame. I suppose he was eighteen when I last saw him. A good person, with a slow humour and a sort of privacy of manner —not secretive, but open and reserved at the same time. There was no quicksilver in his make-up. He did not sparkle: he considered. A certain naïvety, as if he possessed that valuable secret, certainty of the rightness of his own beliefs. He was not beautiful, but handsome, I think, in a solid fashion. After twenty years I can picture him clearly, and he seems older than the others of us, already with the attitude, even to his contemporaries, of a tolerant school-master. Gentle and soft-spoken, physically powerful, compact, on the rugger field and in the Officer Training Corps he was keen, brave, and enviably without doubts or hesitation. I remember he had a friend at school, a constant companion, an older boy, also an athlete, and these two put flesh on another legend for me—the Greek friendship, Achilles and Patroclus. They had that maturity, young men among us boys. If this sounds like hero worship, I give the wrong impression. If it is now, in a way, it was not then. I thought of Roger as somewhat dull, serious and plodding, and so awfully good. You did not talk dirt with Roger—he somehow gave off an atmosphere in which a dirty joke would wither.

One summer—we must have been about seventeen—he and I and several other boys, potential classical scholars, were invited by our classics master to stay with him in Wales for extra coaching. It was a happy time, staying with those *nice* people. (I understand now that one of their attractions to me was that they seemed to have no pretensions, or wishes, to be anything other than what they were. They were sure of their place in 'the scheme of things'.) In the mornings we sat at the dining-table and translated

Greek unseens—Roger Doig, Philip Pendered, Josselyn Hill, Ian Harland, Michael Griggs and I. The master's nickname was 'Crack', though I do not know why. He and his sister led dedicated lives: she to her mother, whom they were tenderly coaxing towards her hundredth birthday; he to the boys of Allenby House, and the pupils of the classical Sixth. Crack had a sort of kindly detachment—the combined influence, you might say, of Greece and Rome. Even then I realized he was impressed by Roger. There was a certain way he looked at him, awed in the presence of such a perfect specimen, and nervous lest some harmful influence damage the still-soft shell. When we all talked of what we were going to do, Roger was silent. But his destiny was as clear to me as if he had been labelled. (I did not know then that Strachey said of Mallory, 'For the rest, he's going to be a schoolmaster, and his intelligence is not remarkable. What's the need?')

In the afternoons we took picnics and walked in the mountains of Snowdonia, to Llanberis and Dwyghifylchi, or on the beaches of Llandudno or Deganwy. Roger walked along the seashore as if conversing with a loose woman: he disapproved of such frivolous pastimes. One whole day was declared a holiday from scholarship in favour of Snowdon itself. We took the mountain simply, walking the easy way up the Pig Track. Even so, I remember feeling at least a little scared at the final scramble over loose stones, with what seemed a sheer jagged drop to the lakes below, bare-edged, cold and opaque as solid turquoise. Roger had climbed silently, with a serious expression. At the summit was a tea-room, a post office and the platform for the rack railway that came up the other side. Several of us decided that we would spend precious pocket-money on riding down on the train. 'How much?' asked Roger sceptically. 'Half a crown.' 'Half a crown! Half a crown for the *ignominy* of going down on the train?'

After school we all had to do two years' National Service.

This was the time of the Korean War. In that limited operation, National Servicemen were not obliged to serve in the combat areas. But Roger, for the highest reasons, from patriotism and a sense of duty, volunteered. He was killed.

As our form master, Crack also taught us English. He would urge us to try to write with a certain classical elegance. As an example of what he required he told us to read — on some days he even cut it out and brought it into class — the fourth leader of *The Times*. This was a somewhat arch, light-hearted little essay, formally witty, a soufflé concocted from nothing, not crudely wisecracking, but amusing, calculated to bring a smile to your lips in the civilized, gentle, English, educated-gentleman manner. I used to read these things in amazement. I did not doubt that what Crack said was true. What schoolmasters said was always true. This must be the way to write English. But was I expected to treat serious affairs — history, politics, letters of condolence — with this calculated frivolity, deflating black thoughts with a sly pun or an apt Latin tag?

Others it seems agreed with me. There is no fourth leader in *The Times* these days. And it has changed in other ways. In another paper, that might not be significant, but in *The Times* it is. It may belong to Lord Thomson, but we believe *The Times*, like the B.B.C., belongs to us. C. P. Scott, the famous editor of the *Manchester Guardian*, said that 'a newspaper is much more than a business: it reflects and influences the life of a whole community; it may affect even wider destinies. It is, in its way, an instrument of government.' Lord Thomson, naturally proud of his expensive pet, has claimed that, 'In many parts of the world *The Times* is Britain; it is the flag.' And on the surface, despite some of the gimmicks of modern journalism, it remains remarkably the same as ever. By selecting the pages, you could believe that the good old days were still with us. The Court Circular announces minor movements of the royal household. Equerries are still accompanying the Royal Family on official visits to R.A.F. stations in Huntingdonshire. The dances and cocktail parties of eligible girls are still ritually listed. Friends of obscure European aristocrats add codicils of personal tribute to the official obituaries. The middle class announce their engagements, in the traditional form.*

Consider: the current editor of *The Times*, appointed by Lord Thomson to coax it into profitable modernity, published, in the euphoria of new fatherhood, an open letter to his infant son. He advised him

> to become an English gentleman – that is 'an independent and kindly man of your word'
> not to seek riches, but to acquire a competence
> enjoy Somerset, the solid foundation of our family life
> ignore fashion, remember that important things do not change. These are God, creative work, love, friendship, comfort and freedom.
> Some physical objects matter – land and Rembrandt and country houses.

This not-quite-endearing list has the true ring of the civilized establishment. Note, in the first admonishment, that peculiar and suspect English insistence on their own honesty.

The Times is not a popular paper, having a circulation of three hundred and fifty thousand only, in a population of more than 55 million (compared, say to the six-million circulation of the *News of the World*, that other truly British paper). But its influence is out of proportion to its circulation. Its correspondence columns are the traditional forum of debate for private citizens, of whatever political persuasion. Trotsky wrote to *The Times*. Graham Greene writes to *The Times*. And always those many minor but

---

* I myself appeared twice in this column. The first announcement produced several offers from photographers and florists but, contrary to popular belief, no flood of circulars offering contraceptives. The second announced that the marriage 'will not now take place'.

important matters that have no other arena for discussion find their way to *The Times*: an extension to the Tate Gallery; a motorway planned to cross ancient parkland. Television, in structure already like an inflated correspondence column, should have supplanted the restricted facilities of newsprint, but it has failed to do so. *The Times* gets about seventy-five thousand letters a year and prints four thousand or so. Recently, tacitly acknowledging that some readers might be less socially adept than in the old days, the name and status of each correspondent appears at the head of the letter. Now we know that a letter signed simply 'H. Legge-Bourke' is from 'Sir Harry Legge-Bourke, Conservative M.P. for the Isle of Ely'. This is useful, since at least half the letters are from men of position: peers (about one letter in twenty), M.P.s, senior officers of the Forces or voluntary organizations or the Church, company directors, well-known individuals. They say the only remaining advantages of a title are the certainty of election to a few exclusive golf clubs and of having your letters printed by *The Times*.

The particular point about the British version of a social elite is that it operates independently of the political structure. It is self-perpetuating and exclusive. The habit of deference was so ingrained in me that, having gained entry to three of the fastnesses of the establishment (public school, Cambridge and a commission in a somewhat patrician regiment), I still had no more notion of naturally belonging than of swimming the Channel. This British establishment has perfected the art of polite ruthlessness. It pretends to change, but beneath the surface it remains the same. Like the Constitution, its rules are unwritten, and that is their strength. Its members can declare that exclusivity is no more, and continue to practise it with all traditional spite. There is no appeal against its decisions: they are made by instinct and conveyed in camera — by nods and smiles and innuendoes.

3. *Go to the Ant*

Go to the ant, thou sluggard! Consider her ways and be wise.

Proverbs vi, 6

I meddle not with any man's conscience. But if by liberty of conscience you mean the liberty to exercise the mass ... it will not be allowed of.

Oliver Cromwell (1599–1658)

Christian: I seek an inheritance, incorruptible, undefiled, and that fadeth not away; and it is laid up in heaven.

John Bunyan, *Pilgrim's Progress* (1678)

Some of the finest qualities of human nature are intimately connected with the right use of money.

Samuel Smiles, *Self-Help* (1859)

I have an old copy of *Pilgrim's Progress*, published in 1825. It is Number Nine in a series of 'Kelly's Elegant Publications', issued in eighteen parts, at sixpence each. Though bound in leather, with gold tooling, it is not an impressive book. Yet evidently it served, instead of a family Bible, as a sacred place of record: 'James Tarrant, His Book,' says the inscription, written out carefully in brown ink, somewhat blotted, 'gave him by his grandfather James Tarrant August 19th, 1865'. Someone—James himself perhaps—has added his second name, Horace, and his date of birth: 'Born June 10th, 1861'. Below are recorded the births of Mary Ann Tarrant, April 24th, 1864, and Albert Tarrant, July 27th, 1867, and elsewhere other family dates and landmarks. On the inside cover is recorded, casually, in pencil: 'Went to Mr Beechey's September 6th, 1874.' I guess the writing is that of James, now thirteen.

This James Tarrant, the recipient, was my maternal grandfather. When I was a child he was already old and almost blind. We visited him rarely, always with a sense of duty and impatience. He lived in a bungalow with his housekeeper, Miss Wing. The rooms, furnished with large heavy pieces of furniture, smelt of old age and mothballs. When Miss Wing went off to Grandad's room to fetch something to show my mother, I would catch a glimpse of his high bulging bed. Grandad and Miss Wing were both small. I believe my picture of Goldilocks in the house of the three bears is related to the memory of those little people among their slightly too large furniture.

Grandad was so nearly blind that he could only recognize

us by our height. So, since we visited him infrequently, he would mistake me, having grown, for my brother. He was a gentle old man, with a smile that seemed to indicate a delight in simple things. I used to watch him openly, knowing he couldn't see me, as he stood up and felt confidently for his pipe on the mantelpiece. We had to take care to leave everything exactly in place, since he knew his way about by touch. I have never reconciled this old man, with his cap of white hair and his gentle manner, with my mother's tales of him, in his nightshirt, firing a shotgun at trespassers from his bedroom window.

Miss Wing too had shining white hair, and a complaining manner. Either she was unhappy with my grandfather, or she did not like my mother. She had some ailment of the hip that made her dip deeply to one side as she walked, and as she busied herself for us, fetching things, bringing tea to the table with its plush cloth, she seemed to bear some resentment. There was always some practical thing that these old people needed help with: changing a mantle in a light (the house was lit by gas-lamps), or disconnecting the accumulator from their precious wireless, so that it could be charged. They were afraid to touch these things themselves.

Out in the narrow garden Grandad had a glasshouse, and a vine in it that bore grapes. He was able to prune it by touch, and thin the bunches of grapes when they formed in the spring. And in our attic once I found a photograph of a magnificent glasshouse of ripe grapes, and my Uncle Bill standing proudly under them. Glasshouses were one of the chief industries of the Lea Valley, and I believe their grapes were well known. But partly too, no doubt, these are common memories of the old times, when fruit came in seasons (a pineapple among the fruit on the sideboard at Christmas was especially significant — an expensive luxury, its mere presence testified a certain achievement) and grapes were not a common import from Greece, Italy,

Spain, France or South Africa ... Why, my mother, I remember, with elaborate care, grew cantaloupe melons, which would only ripen in a good summer. No wonder those childhood days seem to merge, equidistant, with an Elizabethan golden age.

But that copy of *Pilgrim's Progress* is a clue to larger things. As the traditional record book of family history, for my mother's family it had replaced the Bible. Others gave it similar importance. When books were scarce, *Pilgrim's Progress* was both Bible and adventure story. And more: 'with *Rights of Man*,' says the social historian E. P. Thompson, 'one of the two foundation texts of the English working-class movement'. The reason is plain. *Pilgrim's Progress* is indeed the 'classic allegory of Puritan life'. It expounds, directly and without difficult diversion, the Puritan doctrine of deferred reward.

Bunyan's Christian is the apotheosis of Jack Beaver. Or maybe Jack Beaver is the incarnation of Christian. The 'God of Love' is proclaimed, but this love has a stern meaning.* It has the look of duty—duty required from both sides. God appears to take little delight in his creatures, so wilfully disobedient, so reluctant in his worship, so fickle. After those six euphoric days of creation, somehow it has all gone wrong. And for Christian a long and severe path is indicated, beset with obstacles—the Slough of Despond, the Hill of Difficulty, the Valley of Humiliation, the Valley of the Shadow of Death, Vanity Fair, Doubting Castle, the County of Cruelty, the Country of Deceit; and unworthy men—Pliable, Obstinate, Little-Faith, Faint-Heart, Mr Money-Love, Mr Live-Loose, Madam Bubble, Mr Highmind ... to the final joy in the golden streets of the

* One of my school mottoes was: 'Fear God Honour the King'. And, happily, round the dome of the dining-hall ran the passage from *Pilgrim's Progress*: 'Then said He, "My sword I give to him that shall succeed me in my pilgrimage and my courage and skill to him that can get it. My marks and scars I carry with me to be a witness for me that I have fought His battles Who will now be my rewarder." So he passed over and all the trumpets sounded for him on the other side.'

Celestial City, *on the other side* of the Black River of Death.

The message of this belief is simple and quite clear: ignore all distraction. It is a totally practical religion. Its power – or fatal flaw, from the other view – is that the aim of that practicality is indefinite, and therefore suggestible. Without open refutation it can be channelled to political ends. 'There was no *efficient* [my italics] religious idea behind the Roman state,' wrote H. G. Wells, attempting to account for the fall of the Roman Empire. In the name of heaven you may wield great power on earth. 'We teach that only Doers shall be saved': these are the words of the Puritan Thomas Taylor, but the sentiment was common. 'Our rest', said Oliver Cromwell laconically, 'we expect elsewhere.' Bunyan himself, the child of the Puritan revolution, believed we shall be asked to account by a jealous God: 'Were you doers, or talkers merely?' Puritanism is a version of the Ten Commandments, pragmatized for British national ambition.

It was in this atmosphere – both directly, as it was religious, and indirectly, in the general philosophy it inspired – that I was brought up. Its passwords were 'duty' and 'ought'. A religion turned ideology, Puritan ethics consisted of 'moral obligations translated into material terms'. You did things because you should, because they were 'good for you'. What was good for you was work, or at least self-denial. Richard Baxter, an influential seventeenth-century Presbyterian divine, advised the same treatment for religious doubts, moral unworthiness and sexual temptation: a vegetable diet, cold baths and 'Work hard in your calling.' One of the characters in *The Mill on the Floss*, Mrs Glegg, would turn to Baxter's *The Saint's Everlasting Rest* for comfort at times of domestic crisis.

'The Devil makes work for idle hands.' 'Don't just stand there ...' 'You'll live to want.' 'Fine words butter no parsnips.' 'This won't buy the baby a new frock.' 'You're not here to enjoy yourself.' There are many such remarks in the common English vocabulary. It was perhaps not so severe as it sounds, but blind obedience ('Because I *say* so') is certainly part of the Puritan tradition. As God to the parent, so the parent to the child. John Wesley had a very low opinion of the natural character of children. His methods of correcting it were both brutal and unhealthy:

> Let a child from a year old be taught to fear the rod and to cry softly; from that age make him do as he is bid, if you whip him ten times running to effect it. Break his will now, and his soul shall live, and he will probably bless you to all eternity.

By my time that domestic tyranny, which my grandfather at The Green Man no doubt typified, had been tempered by the first indirect news of the psychological revolution. In our house, and in the houses of our friends, practicality had been deified, and it was preached by example.

And the aim of that practicality, which had become an end in itself, was preservation. How daring, almost wicked, must have seemed that Keynesian doctrine of a duty to spend. * Even if it were proved irrefutable it was psychologically impossible. In the broad view, obviously – the sum of private experience that makes national history – this preservation of resources, supported by unceasing hard work, was the reason that the English were so successful in exploiting the first discoveries of the Industrial Revolution. The resources for investment in railways, mines, rubber-planting, shipping, were the available fruits of their self-denial. Yet there again, the final and most important question never seems to be answered: expansion, aggrandizement, development ... for what?

So domestically – the private experience – these attitudes

---

* 'The best guess I can make', Keynes told listeners to the B.B.C. in 1931 – a time of international financial crisis (and the year before I was born) – 'is that whenever you save five shillings you put a man out of work for a day.'

also prevailed. One lesson more than any other was impressed on me: the value of quality, and the false economy of the bargain. A good suit should last a lifetime. If you look after it. Buying the most expensive is a way of relying on the taste of others, why you are unsure of your own. But also this insistence on quality is because possessions are to be preserved. Antiques are the perfect possession: generations have approved their design; time has proved their staying power and enhanced their value. During the war, when money seemed unreliable, my parents began to invest in valuable possessions: a silver teapot, a silver tray, antique glasses and china — instant heirlooms,* appropriate to our socially 'upward mobility'. But these treasures, the 'best' china, the 'best' glasses, the 'best' room, were rarely used. They were 'kept', like girls for marriage. New furniture would not be sat on directly: it was immediately covered with loose covers, themselves protected by 'chairbacks' (antimacassars) and duplicate sleeves fitted on the arms. New cars, similarly, you often see with plastic covers 'protecting' the new seats. I remember the key to the Haylocks' back door was hung on a nail in the kitchen. ('Goodness,' said Mrs Haylock to me one day, 'aren't your hands *white*!' We both understood it as a criticism.) A square of wallpaper matching that on the walls — white worms on a cream ground — was put behind to keep fingermarks from the wall. Elsewhere in the room the wallpaper had faded a little, so that the pro ected square, if uncovered, would be noticeably brighter .. This was the basis of our conservatism — conservation. Left-wing politics, redistributing wealth, were a threat to possessions. All our possessions seemed to be waiting, preserving themselves for that great day when, shamelessly installed in the drawing-room, with the covers off the sofa, antique glasses on the silver tray ... what? The trumpets sound on the other side?

---

* The teapot was engra   d with a sadly prophetic motto: *Non Nobis Solum*— 'Not for us alone'.

Freud made us all amateur detectives of the psyche. We are suspicious and we jump to nasty conclusions. Accumulation of matter, with the sense of pleasing the parent/God figure, reactive tidiness and fastidiousness, the sexual connotations (does not 'spend' mean the release of either money or sperm?)—rubbing our hands together we diagnose a case of arrested anal development. It's inconclusive, but at least it pinpoints a certain unease we have most of us felt about obsessive cleanliness and the exaggerated sense of property. Women are judged ruthlessly by the cleanliness of their houses: the finger slid surreptitiously along the table top, checking for dust. The standard is absolute. A clean home is more important than a warm welcome.

One of the first escape-routes for women from the domestic prison lay in the nursing profession. A profession, it was carefully called, not a job. After the example of Florence Nightingale in the Crimea in the 1850s, nursing became respectable, indeed fashionable, in families where other further education for girls would not have been countenanced. The fashion lasted, start to finish, a hundred years. Now girls regard nursing as a job without glamour. My mother joined it at its mid point, and height. I have a photograph of her with twelve other nursing-sisters, taken in 1919. They look cheerful and capable, with high stiff collars, leg-of-mutton sleeves, laced boots just showing under their long skirts, their hair neatly centre-parted under their bonnets. My mother is evidently one of those lucky girls (she was twenty-four) on whom a uniform sits well: her great white floor-length apron is almost uncreased.

At home my mother ruled her house in a starched white coat, a clinical overall, no doubt inspired by her nursing days. She provided my father with a brown version to wear in the yard. He used to come into the house for mid-morning coffee and sometimes she would persuade him to change into a clean coat before he went out again. We children—my sister and I—home from school for the holidays, would be mooning about, perhaps 'helping' by stringing a basin of currants we had picked from the garden, or shelling peas. My father's coats had removable buttons, fixed with a wire ring, and while he stood at the kitchen table, too hurried even to sit down, my sister or I would change them.

Always to wear a clean coat in the oily workshops evidently required endless trouble. One sensed a conflict with Nature, a fear that, unless controlled, it would burgeon into natural sin. A clean coat, brushed hair, polished shoes, neat gardens, clipped hedges, pruned roses, close-mown lawns with trimmed edges: all demand repeated effort, and are therefore intrinsically virtuous.

The house was spotless. Dust was not given time to settle on the polished table in the dining-room. The net curtains crackled with starch. In our eau-de-nil bathroom, seated on the closed lavatory, Ivy would twist long spears of damp cottonwool and plunge them deep into our ears. We would protest — it was ticklish and painful together. But ears were subject to spot-checks from my mother in the uncompromising north light of the dining-room window. Her medical experience had confirmed a natural antipathy to dirt. She had a brisk way with toilet training, and with all unwanted bodily matter — splinters, germs, nails, pus, blackheads and misplaced hairs. Sometimes the doctor was called in to assist, and they fought a joint campaign. His visit was rather eagerly anticipated, necessitating clean towels in the bathroom and a last-minute wipe round the wash-basin. My mother would inform Dr Harger, or Dr Green, of our symptoms in medical terms — bowels and haematoma and embarrassed breathing, that sort of thing. She would have checked our temperatures before the doctor came, afterwards shaking the thermometer so briskly down to normal I always feared it would snap. Before he left, the doctor and she would hold a consultation in low voices on the landing outside the room.

My father behaved as if he was rather jealous of her intimacy with these doctors. He did not have such a high opinion of the medical profession. He did not go in for medical terms: a strained knee might be 'giving him gyp', rheumatism 'the screws'. He did not like medicines much either. He believed in a 'dose of Eno's' and a certain viscous white mixture, once prescribed for someone else, that he trusted to have an almost magical effect on stomach pains. Otherwise he would have preferred the old-fashioned remedies: hot whisky and lemon, bicarbonate of soda, raw onions, a bread poultice. When, in his last years, he was seriously ill and had a number of pills to take regularly, he used to busy himself about it like an old bear preparing to hibernate, and my mother always had the suspicion that he was actually flushing the useless things down the lavatory.

With so much to be done, there is no time for pleasure. The satisfaction of duty fulfilled has to suffice until it is time for the real reward. The restrictions of marriage, the demands of children, the monotony of dull work, are supported because of this undefined 'duty'. 'Duty' excuses a failure to take a chance, a fear of adventure. There are so many to whom one owes the duty to play safe. To perform all duties is impossible, and failed duty is a reason for guilt. So the avoidance of that guilt ('I have left undone those things that I ought to have done'), the passive joy of not having failed to do your duty, displaces active pleasure. Active pleasure, interfering with the performance of duty, is disapproved of. Thinking what they think they ought to think, these oppressed Christians are nervous even of mental adventure. Physically they become rigid: their lips press together. They have lost the ability to delight in variation. Stability is what matters. Forty years' boredom in the same job, the same house, the same suit, marriage, is, by the marking of time and a certain measure of suffering, more creditable than five years' joy or excitement. Folly, extravagance, irresponsibility, silliness, passion, even unexpected gifts, are an embarrassment. Puritan indoctrination bears a terrible fruit.

Until I was eighteen or so I did not believe my mother had ever been into a pub — I certainly could not visualize her with my grandfather in The Green Man; it was obvious she disapproved of them. One summer day, her father was dying, and my brother and I had driven with her to visit him. On the way back all of us were thirsty and my brother suggested stopping for a drink. 'Yes,' said my mother, 'let's.' And we did. And I believe the incongruity of her presence in that quiet, dusty, pleasant country pub was more in my mind than in hers.

It seems like a regular phase of adolescence to start looking for answers to all the deep questions of existence. But I guess that is because adolescence is when you have the time, and still the hope that you might act out your conclusions. Certainly for me it was a teenage malady. Since I was quite young I had been taken from home on Sundays to church. I remember little of those expeditions. Waltham Abbey was half a mile up the road, and we were always rushed to get there in time — our usual trouble. It seems that it was always cold, and we sat huddled in the shadow of the fat, incised Norman pillars, bored and uncomprehending. Indeed, the vicar contrived to render everything he said, even the Lord's Prayer, almost meaningless by a sort of swooping delivery, ignoring punctuation and descending at random with enormous emphasis on insignificant words — 'Our father which ART in-heaven-hallowed-be-thy NAME ...'

My father never came with us. And the Church was never brought into the house. Attendance was from duty, not choice. At moments of fulfilment (the final preparations for family Sunday lunch) my mother would burst into a couple of lines from a hymn, but we were never told Bible stories or given religious books, as I imagine other children were. Religion, like sex, was a subject too dangerous to discuss.

School did provide religious instruction, in addition to regular services, as it is bound to do by law. Even here, there was a sense that instruction was preferable to discussion, which might lead to embarrassment. At about fourteen I began to want the answers to the fundamental questions that Christianity claimed to be dealing with. What is the purpose of life? I—not the first—wanted to know. I wanted a factual answer: I came from a practical background. Ironically, that puritanical inheritance made me seek answers that the Church could not provide. I could not accept the necessity for an 'act of faith'. I saw no reason why God should not furnish simple proof of his existence. Not to do so was really a cheap sort of trick. That was no way to deal with these important questions. Where was the merit in mystery?

'Fulfil God's purpose,' say the clergy, embarrassed by direct questioning. They fall back on the parable of the talents—general sanctification of human endeavour. They do not want to face the implications of *real* belief. Success, then, is a good use of talents. Calvinists, elevating a simple career to 'a calling', spoke openly of success as 'a measure of grace'; religion acceded to the social contract. To be a 'useful member of society' is sufficient performance of God's requirements: salvation through prosperity, the doctrine of ennobled selfishness, making money for God.

In the chapel at school, a rather large building—a clinical St Paul's Cathedral carved, it seemed when you were inside, from a block of vanilla ice-cream—we were actually admonished by the headmaster for not joining in the Lord's Prayer with greater enthusiasm. It sounded bad, he said, to visitors. I used to think, when he or one of the staff clergy stood in the pulpit and talked about the Kingdom of Heaven and salvation and redemption, why does he have to be so vague? These men themselves must have a vision of the scenery of heaven, of the actuality of God. Even their private opinion would have been encouraging. Blindly I stumbled through Confirmation, emotionally hopeful, confused, dutifully stifling doubt. God and the headmaster had much in common: you did not question their motives.

It is a very English dilemma:

We sat by lamplight opposite one another at a table in his lodgings. He was a fair, aquiline, sensitive young man, with a fine resonant voice, who did his best to keep our conversation away from the business in hand as much as possible. But I was sullenly resolved to make him say — all of it. I asked a string of questions about the bearing of Darwinism and geology on biblical history, about the exact date of the Fall, about the nature of Hell, about Transubstantiation and the precise benefit of the communion service and so forth. After each answer I would say 'So that is what I have to believe ... I see.' I did not attempt to argue. He was one of those people whose faces flush, whose eyes wander off from you and whose voices get higher in pitch at the slightest need for elucidation.

'It's all a little *subtle* you know —' he would begin.

'Still, people might make difficulties afterwards. I want to know what to say to them.'

'Oh — precisely.'

'I suppose it's all right if I just believe this in — er — a spiritual sense.'

'It's much *better* that way. It's ever so much better that way. I'm so *glad* you see that.'

Thus H. G. Wells records his preparation for Confirmation. He was sharper than I. I dutifully memorized the Catechism and answered as required:

Question. Dost thou not think that thou art bound to believe ... ?

Answer. Yes, verily, and by God's help so I will.
Question. What is required of persons to be baptized?
Answer. Repentance, whereby they forsake sin; and Faith, whereby they steadfastly believe the promises of God made to them in that Sacrament.
Question. Why then are Infants baptized, when by reason of their tender age they cannot perform them?
Answer. Because they promise them both by their sureties; which promise, when they come to age, themselves are bound to perform.

Ratify, perform, bound, surety: the Church seems determined to take its pound of flesh.

But Confirmation turned out to be like marriage, virgin sex, the declaration of war, passing forty, a new job: a false Rubicon beyond which all is the same and change still only gradual. In my first term at Cambridge, earnest young men from CICCU (the Cambridge Inter-Collegiate Christian Union), themselves bound for the cloth, infiltrated likely groups and tried to build, kindly but with determination, on the foundation of guilt laid by Confirmation classes and loyalty to the Old School. But I still saw no reason to make an unsupported act of faith. I had a far more basic faith in pragmatism. For that I was able to betray even the Bishop of St Albans, who had laid hands on me at Confirmation. (We were warned not to wear haircream, I remember, out of consideration for His Grace — though even those of us who might have done had learned by then that haircream was only used by spivs.)

Where does it spring from, this Protestant oil and vinegar of evasiveness and direct practicality? Only primitive communities avoid hypocrisy in religion. And the English, with their natural gift for double-think, could be expected to perfect it in their religion. And so we do — in an officially established Church, which we do not allow to meddle in practical matters.

First, that we have granted to God, and by this present charter have confirmed for us and our heirs perpetually, that the English church shall be free, and shall have its rights undiminished, and its liberties unimpaired ... and caused this to be confirmed by Pope Innocent III.

So swore King John, in Magna Carta, nervously protesting his good faith. The independent English were never happy under the authority of Rome. It is their nature to accept authority only for practical reasons, preserving a sort of private arrogance, which causes them to feel confident of being the equal of any man, and probably of God also. Listen to D. H. Lawrence (in *Sons and Lovers*):

'You know,' he said to his mother, 'I don't want to belong to the well-to-do middle class. I like my common people best, I belong to the common people.'
'But if anyone else said so, my son, wouldn't you be in a tear. *You* know you consider yourself equal to any gentleman.'
'I myself,' he answered, 'not in my class or my education or my manner. But in myself I am.'

There is another English paradox, the co-existence in us of pride and humility, self-denial and self-importance, of love equally for freedom and for discipline. This personal privacy — *every* man an island — if any hing can be, is a natural English trait. It springs from a multitude of causes: our geography, our climate, an ancestry of successive invasions of incompatible races. It is a sturdy sort of independence, assuming the right to make decisions for oneself. We are natural democrats. Such men take hardly to the direction of their conscience by venal priests, controlled by a foreign Pope, conducting worship in a scholar's tongue, from a scripture only partly revealed.

Our national mythology has it that Henry VIII broke with Rome for simple sexual reasons: he lusted after Anne

Boleyn and she was holding out for marriage. Out of sympathetic envy for such a robust weakness* he became a folk hero. But actually the English were as ripe for the Reformation as everyone else in Europe. They hated that helpless subjugation to Rome. The papacy was Antichrist itself. In 1821 William Cobbett recalled, 'I most firmly believed when I was a boy, that the Pope was a prodigious woman, dressed in a dreadful robe, which had been made red by being dipped in the blood of Protestants.' Indeed the memory rankles still. Distrust of Catholics runs in Protestant blood. We distrust the worldliness of the Vatican. Apart from the astonishing sexual indulgence of certain notorious Holy Fathers, the papacy in the past has shown too much interest in blatant temporal power. And we suspect that it still does. We also vaguely distrust the Catholic branches of the Royal Family, as if they might still hatch dangerous popish plots. There are rumours: the B.B.C. is run by Catholics; Scotland, beneath the surface proprieties, is split between the masonry of the Catholics and the masonry of Freemasons. What are they teaching in those Catholic public schools? The feeling is rarely explicit (except in Ireland, where Catholics and Protestants are still at one another's throats), but, like residual anti-Semitism, it exists.

The Puritan, stubbornly simplistic, argues that, if you admit to Christian belief, you must wish to live entirely by its teaching. The pure doctrine of Christ is available: to refuse to act on it is to deny your faith. It is an argument of pure, adolescent perfection.

* Henry VIII was not merely the hero-king, bluff and subtle, athletic, musical, a neat poet and brilliant theologian. With equal justice Voltaire described him as 'one of the greatest pests that ever afflicted the earth: brutally despotic, uncontrollable in his rages, barbarous in his amours, homicidal to his wives, a capricious tyrant in affairs of state and religion'. But, though we expect propriety in our current leaders, we prefer the heroes of the past to have had more adventurous lives. A national affection for Edward VII is based almost entirely on his reputation for having been a 'bit of a lad' with Lily Langtry—'the Jersey Lily', Mrs Keppel, 'Skittles', La Belle Otero, and quite a number of other Victorian ladies.

The Puritans were offended by the wanton extravagance of the Renaissance courts. James I they found particularly deplorable. Elizabeth, a sharp and lively ruler, though she gave the impression of magnificence, was not extravagant. Indeed, she was reputedly mean. But James—slyly nick-named 'James Regina'—at the head of a corrupt, extravagant and immoral court, also made 'popish' alliances abroad. He defiantly propounded the divine right of kings: 'As it is atheism and blasphemy to dispute what God can do; so it is presumption and high contempt in a subject to dispute what a king can do, or say that a king cannot do this or that.' The backbone of England, the good country gentry, would not tolerate this nonsense. 'They speak as though they had been brought up all their days on bread and water,' Thomas Nashe said contemptuously of them at the time, 'as though they had been eunuchs from their cradles.' It was these country gentry who inspired the Puritan revolution. In political terms it was not much of a success. In 1649 Charles I was executed. ('I tell you,' said Oliver Cromwell with typical sudden ruthlessness, 'we will cut off his head with the crown on it.') In 1660 the monarchy was restored. Between, a brief victory for a godly cause, and as much cruelty and altercation as under the worst monarch.

But the Puritan revolution was more subtly victorious. As a separate fanatical sect the Puritans did not survive the eighteenth century. But they did, and still do, exert a dreadful influence on the whole of British life. Their victory is to have lost the battle with the Established Church but to have influenced the establishment, both secular and ecclesiastic, more deeply than any victor could have hoped. The extent of their victory lies in the fact that the Church is now almost without influence, but Puritanism is alive in the attitudes of the entire nation. Until very recent years we have been a Puritan country. We are still under Puritan rule. Anyone over thirty, however reluctant, cannot suppress the pangs of residual Puritan guilt.

The secret of the survival of Puritanism within an unsympathetic system lies in its privacy. Whatever the Church may dictate, its children stubbornly insist on a personal interpretation, a personal relationship with God. The private English are naturally attracted to the idea of speaking on a direct line to their Maker, without the clergy listening in on the switchboard. This is Reformation thinking: man *is* an island, reliant on his own will-power, directly responsible to God.

Puritanism is practical. 'The soul of religion', Bunyan's Christian declared, 'is the practical part.' And the accidents of history support the Puritan view: that anal accumulation is justified by periodic wars, depressions, strikes, plagues of locusts, droughts and earthquakes, which draw on those righteously accumulated sources. For those of my parents' generation, the lessons of World War I and the Depression were borne out by the bad times of World War II. Saved by the grace of worldly success—English history echoes with the Puritanical version of Christianity.

For Puritanism is also hypocritical. Even in the brief triumph of Puritan rule men did not really believe that the victories were God's, but Oliver Cromwell's. They expressed it differently: 'God helps them that help themselves.' (The same thought lies behind 'Praise the Lord and pass the ammunition.') One looks to blame someone for the awful inheritance of Puritanism; no one feels like taking responsibility for the faults of his own attitudes. My animosity settles on Oliver Cromwell—though I do not forget that it was the East Anglian yeoman farmers who became his Ironsides. He is somehow to blame for it all. He is indeed one of those figures who seem to stand for more than his own existence. Perhaps as 'the greatest because most typical Englishman of all time'—according to his nineteenth-century biographer, Samuel Newson Gardiner. Being so hypertypically British, Cromwell is no hero to us. But he is irresistibly fascinating; like an eruption on the face of our history, we cannot stop picking at him. Perhaps as the outstanding figure in a critical time—*our* revolution, the first of the great revolutions of modern history, Cromwell really seems to have stood at the crossroads. Andrew Marvell saw him as the personification of the revolution.* Even if it was not true at the time, it has become true now.

A civil war is a national trauma. Cavaliers and Roundheads are our native Cowboys and Indians—they survived until recently as useful divisions for boys' games. *The Children of the New Forest*, a very sentimental version of history, was one of the three or four favourite books of my childhood.† But the Civil War was that paradox, a domestic conflict. A local Warwickshire squire, setting out one Saturday in 1642 for a day's hunting, to his surprise encountered the king at the head of his army. Until that moment he was quite unaware of the war. But he did not hesitate. He turned back his hounds, shut them in the kennels, summoned his tenants, changed his clothes and joined his king. Next day, after the Battle of Edgehill, the king knighted him.

Cromwell was gentry, from a country family with good connections. When he entered parliament there were seventeen of his relations also on the benches. From such a privileged station he was the champion of equality. Parliament, he said, must be predominant, since it alone represented the 'plain people'. Yet he had the traditionalists' desire to see a settlement of England's troubles 'with something of monarchical power in it'.

---

* Admittedly Marvell was Cromwell's Secretary at the time, and rather eager to please: his 'Horatian Ode' contains these wooden lines:

> And if we would speak true
> Much to the man is due.

Elsewhere of Cromwell, he wrote this marvellously guarded praise:

> If these be the times, then this must be the man.

† The others: *Twenty Thousand Leagues Under the Sea*, *Swiss Family Robinson*, *David Copperfield*—the fruits of chance accumulation on my parents' shelves.

At the outbreak of the revolution Cromwell was forty-three, an age when lack of achievement may turn to frustration and violence. This, together with the certainty of his own grace, made him an impatient spirit, growing to arrogance and cruelty. He dissolved his parliament three times because it acted against what he *knew* was right — 'and God judge between you and me.' Yet he was inconsistent, at times deeply melancholy, at times wildly boisterous. 'Lord, though I am a miserable and wretched creature, I am in covenant with Thee through grace.' The Lord's will, which was known to Cromwell, excuses all — even the execution of a king: 'The providence of God has cast this on us.' At times, in that precarious relationship of 'sanctimony and sadism', his fervour was bloodthirstily cruel. The massacres of the Irish contaminate us still: 'You must all of you have blood to drink; even the dregs of the cup of the fury and wrath of God.'

Cromwell was a family man, who found time to dine with his wife and daughters, however pressing the affairs of state. A man of deep, almost ecstatic piety. A practical man: 'Truly I believe he that prays best fights best.' He trained his New Model Army on prayer and fierce discipline. A hardworking, patriotic, dutiful man, slow to take an argument but mule-stubborn when his mind was made up. A country man, a great fancier of horseflesh, with Arabs from Aleppo and Barbaries from Tripoli, and more elegant coach-teams than any monarch ever had. A lover of hawks and hounds and deer; a rural weekender — from Friday to Monday at Hampton Court he amused himself with the construction of fishponds and rabbit warrens. A plain man, with his puffy, flushed, determined face. When he first entered parliament he was 'very ordinarily apparelled'. Asked to identify him, John Hampden forecast: 'That sloven will be the greatest man in England.'

Twenty years later, on April 20th, 1653, Cromwell, in a plain black suit and grey stockings, took his usual seat in parliament. There were about fifty members present, distributed on the benches that ran round three sides of the hall, with the Speaker in the middle, raised above them on his high seat. Cromwell had been warned what was going on. This parliament was about to hear the third reading of a Bill that, in simple terms, guaranteed its own perpetuity. For half an hour Cromwell listened to the speeches, with mounting anger. Then, 'This is the time,' he said to his companion, Thomas Harrison, 'I must do it.' He took off his hat and began to address the House, at first earnestly and reasonably. But his impatience, his anger and his outrage got the better of him. He began to criticize members personally. They objected. Cromwell, furious now, gave his tongue free rein. 'It is not fit that you should sit as a parliament any longer. You have sat long enough, unless you have done more good.' He was shouting now, striding up and down the raised floor at the centre of the House. He put his hat back on his head: he had no respect for such a shameful assembly. Marten was a whoremaster. Wentworth an adventurer. Challoner a drunk. Another a thief. Another a cheat. He turned on Vane, the instigator of this infuriating Bill. He stamped his foot. He called him a juggler with common honesty. 'It's you that have forced me to do this,' he cried, 'for I have sought the Lord night and day that he would rather slay me than put me upon the doing of this work.' He was beside himself with righteous anger. He snatched the Bill up from the clerk's table below the Speaker's seat. 'I will put an end to your prating. You are no parliament. I say you are no parliament. I will put an end to your sitting. Call them in. Call them in.' He had brought with him from Whitehall thirty musketeers. They filed into the chamber. 'This is not honest,' protested Vane. 'It is against morality and common honesty.' 'Oh Sir Henry Vane! Sir Henry Vane!' cried Cromwell. 'The Lord deliver me from Sir Henry Vane!'

Less than a year later, in a suit of chestnut brown embroidered with gold, Cromwell drove in state to a banquet given in his honour by the City of London. The cannon at the Tower fired a salute. He was given a handsome gift of plate. He knighted the Lord Mayor, and went home in torchlight procession. In that same year it was declared treason to talk ill of Cromwell. 'What if a man take upon himself to be king?' he once tentatively asked. Now the Protector had become dictator. Before long, England had become a police state, riddled with spies, ruled by local commissars – Cromwell's Major-Generals. The press was severely censored: only two papers were allowed. There was even talk of taking all Irish children from their parents at the age of ten, to be indoctrinated in 'industry and protestantism'. No wonder some have joined Cromwell's name with Hitler's.

'An egregious dissembler and a great liar.' 'The most absolute single-hearted man in England.' It is his arrogant abasement that gives the clue to the paradox of Cromwell's character: 'Truly I have been called unto them by the Lord and therefore am not without some assurance that he will enable his poor worm and weak servant to do his will and fulfil my generation.' There it is, in that revolting statement: Cromwell believed he was, as we his heirs are so often urged to do, serving God's purpose on earth.

After his death Cromwell's corpse was dug up and hung at Tyburn, and his head impaled on a pole outside parliament. But it was too late. God had finally been discredited.

At the Restoration Anglicanism officially replaced Protestantism. And now still the Church remains, established, formally acknowledged, but disregarded. *The Book of Common Prayer* is actually the schedule to an Act of parliament. Most people give the Church the sort of attention they would pay an ailing relative: it is women's work, a duty to be performed only so far as it is not too intrusive. The Church no longer has the power to call the tune. Humiliated, and somehow pathetic, it takes the lead from society, provides a useful place to demonstrate social events: births, deaths, marriages, remarriages.* Since it is established it is paid lip-service, literally, with a daily act of Christian worship in schools prescribed by Act of parliament. Dogma itself is tactfully sidestepped: in a recent syllabus, for instance, London teachers were encouraged to concentrate on comparative studies of Judaism, Islam and Hinduism; to prefer the safer ground of the New Testament to the Old; and to 'play down' the magic of the miraculous. 'Christian' almost ceases to have a religious meaning. A Minister of Education speaks of forming immigrant children – Indians, Pakistanis, Jamaicans – into a 'civilized Christian community'.

The duty to God, in such an established religion, merges into, and is eventually lost in, a duty to the community. The duty, instilled by threats of Hell, promises of eternal bliss and gifts of absolution, was promoted by a Christian-dominated education hopeful of setting up a self-perpetuating social rhythm. But no motion is perpetual; and now it is almost run down. Statistics again: 65 per cent of the British, according to a Gallup Poll, believe that the Church should keep out of politics and should not express itself on these or any other social matters.

As children we used to be taken on day-trips to the nearest seaside, to Frinton on the north Essex coast. In those days Frinton was a notoriously snobbish resort. Coaches were not allowed in the town (this is still the case – nor are there any pubs in the town), and on the sands there were almost as many nannies as children. The snobbery was middle-class pretentiousness. The really grand did not go away 'on holiday', or stay in hotels. Once we went to stay in Frinton ourselves. We made friends with a family in the same hotel and we went about with them most of the time.

---

* To put statistics on it, 50 per cent of the population is married in church, and 75 per cent buried under its auspices. One in eight goes to church once a month. Fifty per cent of children are baptized. But less than two million take communion even once a year – and that is a drop of more than 10 per cent in ten years.

After dinner we would all meet for coffee in the lounge. It was usually time for me to go to bed then. One evening, for some reason, I felt embarrassed about kissing my mother goodnight, in front of these strangers, and this girl, and I was going off without doing so, when the man said in a disapproving tone, 'Aren't you going to kiss your mother goodnight?' So I defiantly said that I wasn't. There was no reason for this. But his disapproval made the idea even more embarrassing. Next day my mother told me seriously that he had been 'shocked' that I had not said goodnight to her 'properly'. That tiny scene is Cromwell's fault. That man, and I, and my mother with her concern over other people's opinion, we were all acting out our Puritan inheritance.

I see the dying influence of Puritanism in a hundred British attitudes. In the British habit of social obedience – we are a law-abiding people. In plain English food. And plain English names: we children were christened Peter, John and Ann – you cannot get plainer than that. I see Puritanism in the horror of charity and the tendency to starve rather than undergo a means test. I see it in the guilty compulsion to work (or at least guilt when not work-ing). In the intolerance of deviation, of all different be-haviour. In the tendency to fasten on the one fault, no matter how much surrounded by beauty. In such small things as the dislike of long hair – 'the unloveliness of lovelocks'. In the conception of art as decoration only, never as the central thing. In the reluctance to alter restric-tive laws – on licensing hours, for instance, or Sunday entertainment. In the conception of work as toil that, if enjoyable, ceases to be honourable. In the need for the security of possessions. In prudery, in sexual repression in the name of modesty, in the hysterical envy of sexual pleasure. In the arrogant interference with others' con-science, whereby a man has not the right to decide on his own suicide. In the automatic and nervous disapproval of everything new. The horror of lack of inhibition. The fear of spontaneity. All the wrong things for the right-sounding reasons: because it is good for you, because it is *right*, because it always *has* been. In the Samuel Smiles doctrine of self-improvement.* In the building-society motto, 'Save and Prosper'. Even in that sincere atheism of the 'twenties and 'thirties when British intellectuals sought in Marxist ideology an unselfish purpose in life. ('They are still smarting', said George Orwell in 1947, 'from the failure of Communism as God.' God is not the only god that failed.) I see Puritanism in the style of the labour movement, and in the trade unions. In all politicians, indeed, who call on us to work for 'a new Britain', to 'invest in the future', and hail knuckling under to the system as 'a triumph of common sense'. I see it in my father's passionate attacks on parasitic plants: ivy and woodbine and nettles roused him to fury. I see it in the fear of displaying more than a certain accepted proper show of affection, of revealing true feelings. In the tyranny of 'What will people say?' — recalling the babysitter who would not be dropped at the door of her house: though married she did not wish to be seen by the neighbours being dropped home late at night by a succession of strange men. It is there in *flagrante delicto*, meaning as it does to most people — flagrantly enjoying themselves. In 'Never speak ill of the dead.' In the disapproval of 'irregular hours', either in work or leisure. In the notion of 'keeping yourself' for another person, implying as it does their right to possession. Even in that guilty lip-service to the Church ... Cromwell lives.

---

* *Self-Help* was published in 1859, the same year as Darwin's *Origin of the Species* and John Stuart Mill's *Essay on Liberty*. *Self-Help* was reprinted seventy-five times and translated into twelve languages. Smiles followed it with *Character* (1871), *Thrift* (1875) and *Duty* (1880). His message, in his own words, was that 'nothing creditable can be accomplished without application and diligence.' 'We often think we are being educated,' he said, 'while we are merely being amused.'

4. *One Noble Subject*

I don't know why anyone should waste his time and beat his head about the Latin grammar, who does not intend to be a critic, or make speeches and write dispatches in it.
John Locke, *Some Thoughts Concerning Education* (1693)

> And we all praise famous men—
> Ancients of the College;
> For they taught us common sense—
> Tried to teach us common sense
> Truth and God's Own Common Sense,
> Which is more than knowledge!
> Rudyard Kipling, *Stalky & Co.* (1899)

If ever in after life your job is to think, render thanks to Providence that, for five years of your youth, you did a Latin prose once a week and daily construed some Latin author.
A. N. Whitehead, *The Aims of Education* (1932)

You also have gentlemen in England. I've never met a gentleman from any other country. He's a wonderful specimen of humanity.
Henry Miller, 1969

In Britain education and class have grown inextricably entwined. Despite the false dawn of Angry Young Men in the 'fifties, this is still the case. It grows less important by slow degrees, but private education—what we perversely call public schools—does still create a socially ambitious class that emulates, and so supports the habits and attitudes of the establishment.

In 1968 the Public Schools Commission, set up by an uneasy government, reported on two hundred and eighty-eight of these schools. It roundly declared them socially divisive. Ninety per cent of places in boarding schools are taken by the sons of men officially ranked as upper class.* Not surprisingly so, if that also means richer, since it costs on average more than five hundred pounds a year in board and tuition fees alone to send a boy to public school.

At the age of fourteen, say, 3 per cent of all boys are at these schools. And almost half of them go on to university. More significantly, 45 per cent of undergraduates entering Oxford and Cambridge come from independent schools. Over half the men in senior grades of the civil service come from public schools—that is, from less than 3 per cent of the available talent. A public-school manner is still a necessary qualification for entry into certain professions. Seventy-one per cent of the directors of the two hundred largest British companies are Old Boys ...

Private education is a spanner in the systems of the country. It feeds the middle-class snobberies and dishonesties.

* The Registrar General has us classed thus: 1—Professional; 2—Managerial; 3—Skilled non-manual; 4—Semi-skilled; 5—Unskilled.

Its morality is superficially that of Christian self-denial, but beneath that is a deep and ruthless selfishness. Disciplined to conformity, its products are the Pretorian Guard of the establishment. It is, indeed, 'not as bad as it was', and lately has adopted a more modern style, but while admission is controlled by wealth, it necessarily has a special clientele.

The circle has to be broken by government action. Yet even a Labour government, with enormous popular sympathy, hadn't the courage to take it. And it is for such surgery that government exists. While the systems continue, the alternatives are deprived of the talent that has been creamed off. 'The dilemma for the progessive parent is that he does not want to jeopardize his child's material future, but neither does he want the child to be a Freemason or a member of Lloyd's.' Maurice Punch (a sociologist at the University of Essex) put the dilemma exactly. Hundreds of middle-class parents consider the problem of elitist education with distaste, and end up sending their children to private schools, to give them the advantage of smaller classes, personal interest from the staff, out-of-school friendships and activities. Like drunken drivers, they wish the government would force them to do what they feel is right.*

By a sort of logical paradox, for some of us a public school provides the chance of social mobility. Our parents, 'upwardly mobile' in the jargon of sociology, were themselves too old to be trained, but they were able to buy this social ladder for their children.

With perverse luck, my schools were exactly true to the famous types. Evelyn Waugh, I can tell you, exaggerated only by a breath in *Decline and Fall* (1928). In 1939 I was seven. I think my parents' doubts about private education were purely financial. Fresh salmon and prep-school education were in the same category: if you could afford it you had it. There were anxious consultations with the Wattses

---

* I find myself in this position.

and the Sweetenhams. (Mr Haylock had no doubts about private education either: a presumptuous waste of money, pampering children who should be able to get by on hard work. Mr Haylock was John Bull too.)

The most difficult step in private education is the first. Knowing where to start is the nerve-wracking problem. Once within the system you can be passed round by personal recommendation. It's a small world. The same French teacher, a Miss Rathkins—we called her 'Ratskins'—turned up to teach my sister several years after she had been teaching at my school. What's more, in 1939 war was evidently imminent. In the end I was sent to a school in Devon, where the Watts's son was also going, safely distant from the threat of bombs in London. I heard Chamberlain's broadcast telling us we were at war, in the living-room of the Sweetenhams' cottage, and I seem in my memory actually to have been on the way to Devon at the time.* In any case, it can only have been days apart.

That school was a disastrous choice. The headmistress (if there was a headmaster she quite overshadowed him) was mad. Eccentric, if you like. Her habitual tone of voice was a shout. She tried to jolly us out of homesickness by shouting fearsome tales of her own childhood when she came to turn out the lights in the dormitory. The more sensitive boys suffered nightmares or waking terrors.

When my parents left I wept, but ceased after a day or two. My mother told me later that Mrs Engelheart had commended my bravery. 'Plucky little fellow,' I expect she said. But actually I had started badly. On the first night I had to get up and go to the lavatory. I knew only roughly where it was. It was pitch dark. I felt my way along the dormitory, out into the passage. It was becoming desperate. I found the lavatory, but still not the light-switch. By the

* In fact, I *remember* that the broadcast was made by Churchill, but history has it otherwise. Apparently I was one of many moving to 'safe' areas. More than three and a half million moved in the two months to September, and a quarter of the population in September itself.

time I did it was too late: I had thoroughly messed my pyjamas. I can recall that horror vividly. For some reason my
bed was in the centre of the dormitory. I lay miserably in
those pyjamas for the rest of the night. In the morning, desperate to dispose of them, I feebly hid them under the
mattress. When the cleaner discovered them, I was hauled
back to account for myself. And I was treated kindly, when
I had believed it to be an unforgivable crime.

Otherwise I remember little of that place except Mrs
Engelheart, her red hair, her fierce Siamese cats, the pea-
cocks in the grounds, screaming at first light. And 'cream
teas'* in the Arundell Arms, the local hotel, where visiting
parents stayed and gorged their boys and their boys' friends,
inarticulate in their Sunday suits. I do not remember the
classrooms. Was it here or at another school that I was para-
lysed by nerves in the middle of a piano piece at the school
concert? My schooldays were regularly punctuated by such
ordeals.

After two terms in Devon my parents took me away. It
was safe from raids, but otherwise the inadequacies were too
obvious to ignore. I next attended another doomed establishment. Its premises were requisitioned at the beginning of
the war for some national purpose, and the school moved,
surviving with difficulty, to a village in Hertfordshire. The
longest village in the county, we were told it was—a fact
easily believed once we had walked most of its length in
crocodile to church and back on Sunday. For two or three
years the school staggered on. In the last term there were
less than twenty pupils.

That house seemed vast to me then. I remember the
dining-room, large and airy, with bare board floors, where I
first encountered syrupy, green tomato jam, and marrow
jam too (rationing had certainly reached Hertfordshire). I

---

* Cream teas are West Country food—another local survival. And because no one
wants scones and jam and whipped cream in the middle of a working day, they have
become holiday food. In 1939 only the letter of rationing had reached Devon, not
yet the fact.

remember the grounds where we collected Spanish chestnuts to roast on the stove in the hall. (The trick was to lay them against the mica windows of the fire just before class started, and ask to 'be excused' ten minutes later. But did I ever dare to do this, or merely admire other boys who did?) I remember the park, where we were allowed to walk, with permission, in pairs.

On the gravel forecourt of the house the headmaster bade farewell to parents fetching boys at the end of term. 'Goodbye,' said Mr Macdonald, leaning in the car window one summer afternoon. 'The same to you with knobs on,' said my sister, who had just learnt the expression at school. Later it was a family joke, but at the time true English embarrassment seized the whole family. I do not believe Mr Macdonald was in the least perturbed. He later gave my sister a mongrel puppy (fathered by an Airedale on the Macdonalds' Labrador). We called it Nigger.

In those days I was a high-spirited but obedient pupil. Dressed in sacking I acted the title role of Cinderella in a pantomime for the parents. I nervously forgot the lines, and ad-libbed feebly. In the interval a master read out a piece he had written, a little piece that incorporated the names of all the boys and staff. Having ingeniously included me in a sentence about a school holiday (' ... and there was KNOW-LERning ... ') he ruined it both times – there was an encore – by saying '*Knowler-erning*'. Despite a school career dogged by howlers,* other people's small imperfections have always irritated me.

The scab of my smallpox vaccination (on my thigh – my

* In the margin of my Latin verses would be scrawled '*φεῦ! φεῦ!* Look at *cordes!*' ('Few, few', in our pronunciation: the Greek tragic cry of woe. 'Cordes', for non-classicists, is a masculine plural ending on a neuter noun. Latin, and Latin verses in particular, was like a crossword puzzle, fitting words in measured feet instead of squares. If you ever forgot the pattern of hexameter and pentameter you could run through this unforgettable couplet:

— ∪∪ — — — ∪∪ — — — ∪∪ —
Down in a/deep dark/dell sat an/old cow/munching a/turnip/
— ∪∪ — — — ∪∪ — ∪ — ∪∪ —
Out of its/mouth came/forth/breakfast and/dinner and/tea.

sister and I were vaccinated together and had it in this feminine position to be alike) was coming loose. In bed after lights
out, I touched it warily. It felt as large as a penny. Opposite
the dormitory was the Macdonalds' bedroom. Mrs Macdonald was giggling. Something was going on in there that
I could comprehend only by instinct. The scab came off. It
was exciting. Carefully I preserved it till morning. In the daylight it was a tiny dark piece of dried matter.

When the school closed Mr Macdonald had the happy
idea of letting each boy choose a book from the library. I
have mine still, like a stone preserved from a demolished
building. With unerring luck (I believe I made the choice
from its appearance) I chose that most English of books, an
edition of *Handley Cross** with illustrations by John Leech.

But actually my memories of that place are false. Recently
I was in the village and I walked up the drive to the house.
It is not very large, and badly crumbling. The forecourt is
a small area of mossy gravel, the grounds overgrown, the
lawn under two feet of hay. Dirty curtains were drawn
across the windows. No one came to the door when I rang,
but an old dog barked and leapt between the curtains and
the window. It was frightening to see such decay. That window at which the dog leapt was the window of the top form.
There was a very fat boy, I remember, whom I would taunt
until he chased me round the table ...

My next school, in Buckinghamshire—the third and last
of my prep schools—had a more prosperous air. It was
shabby, but a going concern. Some of the masters were in
the Forces and there were ladies temporarily in their place.
But the headmaster, white-haired and urbane, had that un-
worried air of a true gentleman.

He was also a classical scholar. That fact shaped my life
for the next ten years, and ultimately longer. With Rousseau

---

* Or *Mr Jorrocks's Hunt*. I didn't know what I had then, but I now enjoy
the Victorian story of this bumptious grocer, with his cries of 'Werry rum!' and
'Dash my vig!'—a Pickwick figure, but mercilessly vulgar, and doubtless another
version of my John Bull grandfather. I see from the inscription that this was 1943.

in this at least, I 'was taught Latin and all that useless stuff'. For the first two periods every morning—while the brain was fresh, he said—Mr Evans had the Sixth Form for Latin. The half-dozen potential scholars were started on Greek. We had these lessons from a man who lived in the village, and we walked to his house to save him coming to the school. We sat at his dining-table, with french windows to the garden. He did not seem like a teacher. A smiling, avuncular man, he was endlessly patient, never pressing us to learn, never critical that we had forgotten what last week he had so carefully explained. I believe he was not well and had to take things quietly. Indeed, from time to time it was we who had to rouse him from his reverie. In the autumn he would tell us, as we left, to pick a few apples for ourselves from the garden.

They say that learning is easy at that age. I think it was. In those few years I accumulated a hump of classical knowledge on which I lived, more and more sparsely, for ten years. Much of it was simply learned by heart. Mr Evans distributed a printed sampler of sentences that illustrated the use of the Latin conditional and a number of idiomatic phrases. I fixed mine with stamp hinges at the front of *Kennedy's Latin Primer*. Some I remember still: *Si hoc facies injuste ages* and *Si foret in terris rideret Democritus.** These were intended to convince examiners of your intimacy with the Ciceronian style. In scholarship exams, both to public school and to Cambridge, I stuffed my proses with as many of these phrases as I could. It seemed to work. But my knowledge of the classics was never more than nervous respect. I had no basic understanding, just a certain superficial knowledge. With French and English I felt to be among friends, but with Latin I put on parlour manners, applying a set of received rules, with no sense of feeling the right and wrong of a language. And all the time that sense of danger,

* 'If you do this you will do wrong,' and 'If Democritus were on earth he would laugh.'

working in the dark with electric cables, half expecting a false connection and φεῦ! φεῦ! Look at *cordes*!

Indeed, the whole system of exams was another example of the English preoccupation with appearances. The aim was to *appear* to know as much as possible. Co-operation between you and your teachers to discover what you best could or would like to do was not to be considered. Was not Mr Evans a successful teacher? Under that system there is no doubt he was. Yet I never learnt to read Homer without the sense that I was working at translation, never with the sense that I could appreciate it as writing. I acted in the Greek play at Cambridge ignorant of much of what the other characters were saying: I was still using the knowledge learnt by heart from Mr Evans. In my last year at Cambridge I changed subjects. It turned out to be only in the nick of time: my tutor told me they would have taken my scholarship away. I do not think that this dying interest in the classics was my fault – or indeed theirs, I suppose. There simply never had been, in a way in which I did not have to feel defensive, the opportunity to discuss whether this was the subject I wanted to do. I was a classical scholar, and there was no question of abandoning that.

The classics, they say, train the mind. 'The mind requires healthy exercise,' wrote Edward Thring, headmaster of Uppingham, in 1867. 'The end product is strength of mind and it is a matter of complete indifference, provided the result is true, whether the years of practice and preparation are full of immediate gain or not.' 'Let the mind', he said, 'be educated in one noble subject ... the study of Latin and Greek literature.'

Others though had a clearer idea of the practical applications of Latin: 'We must go to Rome for our lessons,' wrote Sir Richard Livingstone in 1917. 'To govern people who differ in race, language, temper and civilisation; to raise and distribute armies for their defence or subjection, to meet expenses civil and military; to allow generals and governors sufficient independence without losing control at the centre; to know and supply the needs of provinces two thousand miles from the seat of government ... Latin then stands in our education partly on linguistic grounds, partly on the heroic characters in its history, on the interest of its political and imperial problems, and the capacity of its peoples for government.' When, with the decline of the power of the Church, in education* and in public affairs, the classics were less exclusively her privilege, it turned out to be possible to find in Greece and Rome inspiration for all the imperial attitudes of expanding Britain. William Blake had already pointed to this trend, in 1818, admonishing Gibbon and others for making heroes of Alexander and Caesar. 'The Classics! It is the Classics and not Goths nor Monks that Desolate Europe with Wars!'

The classical world became the fantasy ideal. The nobility of Rome, the conception of *gravitas*, somehow merged with the aesthetic and subtle (i.e., dishonest) Grecian manner, providing an ideal prototype of the imperial adventurer. Cecil Rhodes, imperialist visionary, was pleased to know that he resembled Hadrian. 'In the thousand years which followed the birth of Christ,' wrote Lord Asquith, 'there was no era in which the external conditions of life were so favourable to the happiness of mankind as the reign of the Emperor Hadrian.' Like our similar vision of a robust Elizabethan paradise, this view of Rome was false and one-eyed.

'The disciplinary value [of Latin] is its greatest educational asset.' This is not the pronouncement of a Victorian headmaster, but of the Incorporated Association of Assistant Masters in 1962. The old attitudes survive. In the 1870s Eton had thirty-one masters: twenty-six taught classics, six mathematics, and one history. In 1970 there were

---

* Though, in 1872, seventy out of seventy-two headmasters of the leading schools were ordained clergy. When London University was founded in 1828 as a nonsectarian foundation, it was attacked as 'that godless institution in Gower Street'.

twenty-three masters teaching classics, eighteen science, fifteen maths, and thirty-one English and modern languages.

Rules, and therefore discipline, are the basis of public-school education. Even progressive teachers find themselves at odds with parents ambitious for their children's success. Teaching by rule has to them been proved to be effective. A knowledge of Latin, for instance, seems common to many men they would wish to emulate — doctors, judges, headmasters, statesmen, diplomats. These parents, socially besieged, do not want to run the risk of change that might further erode their status. Their defence is to raise the drawbridge and hope it will all blow over.

Within the castle, choice is eliminated by rules, safely hallowed by tradition. Even English composition was taught us by rules. Miss Lee, delicate and prim, taught us at that school in Buckinghamshire. We learnt the named grammatical parts of language, as if by naming each bone in your finger you will become more skilful with your hands. There were words we were forbidden to use, words that were intrinsically wrong, whatever the context. 'Nice', for instance. The first person. 'Got.' 'Things.' I can see what she was getting at, but Miss Lee never felt the need to explain it at the time. The rule was sufficient. And her manner did not encourage discussion. Under her dainty exterior she had nerves of steel. We used to watch her cross the park (she lived in one of the lodges), stepping fastidiously through the common vegetation. One morning she fell while negotiating the stile. At the window of the Sixth Form, waiting for her to take our next lesson, we laughed: that dignity of hers needed upsetting. After a pause she rose slowly and gracefully from the ground, and continued. But she did not come straight to the classroom. She had broken her wrist.

Many of the public-school rules are unwritten, expressed in such sayings as 'Play the game,' 'Don't let the side down,' 'Keep a straight bat.' They are intended to create a type, easily recognizable, loyal to the group, and 'keen'. Rules extend to personal matters. In my day, fashionable clothes were disapproved of. Haircream was despicable. ('Groisy' was the ultimate condemnation. 'Groise' was slang* for butter or any other fat. The pats of fat we had at meals were groise, and foreigners and, I suppose, Jews would be called 'groisy'.) And the discipline is not merely temporary. The Old Boy Net enters the language ('I say, old boy ... ') because it exists. And the Net has its rules also. We knew we were 'not allowed', as Old Boys, to wear suede shoes when returning to school on a visit. You would wear your old school tie to an interview if you thought it might be recognized.

When I was at school the drawbridge mentality was quite deliberately practised. The outside world was either excluded or ruthlessly falsified. Certain papers were banned (but how we fell on the *Sunday Dispatch* when it serialized *Forever Amber*!). The cinema was out of bounds, but selected films were shown in Big School on Saturday evenings (as I remember it, it seems that *The Crossing of Antarctica* and *Blithe Spirit* were shown in permanent rotation). The school magazine, though written mainly by the boys, was heavily censored by one of the masters, who maintained that criticism of a school function was a criticism of the master who had organized it, and that was a criticism of the headmaster who had appointed him, and that, naturally, was out of the question. The only girls you saw were sisters—your own or others'.

Aware of some dissatisfaction with this severance from the outside world, our headmaster—C.P.C., or 'Sheepy' Smith—once preached a sermon on the philosophy of this education. Its purpose, he told us, was to instil at this formative stage standards that would be the foundation of adult life. While the boys, therefore, were still malleable, they

---

* Other random examples: 'mingy' = mean, 'tool' = penis, 'S.E.T.' (sliced elephant's tool) = sliced cold meat, 'White City' = the communal-lavatory complex (roofed, but partly open-air), 'smooth' = sexually attractive little boy, 'hags' = matrons, 'squit' = new boy, etc.

were not to be exposed to 'bad' influences. I do not doubt his sincerity, but I do doubt the value of his results. Apart from the fact that it turns education into a process of moulding, not of development, its standards are pretty much on the surface — a morality of manner * and not of spirit. Educated to believe that everyone acts from the highest principles, the sudden exposure to business ruthlessness very often acts as a stimulant. All that tough, virile dealing seems glamorous and exciting. It would never seem so if the fact of it had been commonly discussed during those formative years.

At the time I was being processed, a friend of my parents said approvingly, 'You can always tell a public-school boy by the way he comes into a room.' In recent years the type has grown his hair rather longer, and toned down his mannerisms, but he is still recognizably the brother of the type of my generation. That type was confident, but it was a shallow confidence, functional only on its own ground. The application of accepted rules saved him the need to think things out for himself. He was sexually inhibited, Conservative, patriotic, royalist. His natural habitat was the City, the golf club, Surrey, Buckinghamshire, Sussex. He was beginning to feel besieged within these preserves and was apt to blame it all on the socialists. He believed in doing one's best, self-control, and behaving like a gentleman.

Public schoolboys form a secret society within society. The old school tie is that society's Masonic handshake. Like Masons, faithful to their own kind, in the small things they are honest, but in the basic encounters hopelessly deceptive, though not always intentionally. The amazing affair of Kim Philby, protected by class and education even when evidently suspect as a spy, was a triumph of the Old Boy Net. Who could believe that those public schoolboys,

* Winchester, probably the first public school, was founded in 1382 by William of Wykeham. Hence Old Boys of that school are known as 'Wykehamists'. This is an important piece of middle-class general knowledge. William gave the school its famous motto: 'Manners Makyth Man.'

Burgess and Maclean, so noticeably suave when entering a room, were actually traitors? It is tempting to declare it could never happen again. That triumphal affair should have been at the same time the death-rattle of those out-dated values. But these things that could never happen again, they have the habit of happening again.

Public-school morality, that particular form of self-interested chivalry, was most directly inspired by Greece and Rome, rediscovered to colour the expanding British Empire with a certain historical glamour. Britain had actually been put through the Roman Imperial mill; it had an effect on the straightness of our roads, but otherwise clearly we retained a slumbering respect for the Ancient manner. School rules sought to reimpose this style, with Ciceronian debating societies and administrative rigidity. The school prefect system is a Spartan imitation. 'Hands out of your pockets!' they shouted at us; 'Keep your hands under your cloaks,' was the Spartan version. Spartan prefects carried whips; ours had their canes. Spartan boys went barefoot; we had to jump into a cold bath before breakfast. *Victor ludorum*, silver cups instead of Olympic vases, obedience, discipline, unquestioning loyalty ... Even the book plates in school prizes were printed in Latin: I seem to have won, in 1950, the Hudson Prize for Latin Prose: *Hunc Librum*, it says, *Diligentiae Praemium*. The battle of Waterloo may have been won on the playing-fields of Eton, but Eton itself was founded on the battlefield of Thermopylae. Over the dead from that battle was written:

> Go tell the Spartans, passer-by
> That here, obedient to their laws, we lie.

And just in case we had been defeated at Waterloo, it is also an important part of that education to learn to be a 'good loser', to accept defeat with a good grace.

The Reform Act of 1867 gave urban workers the vote. Robert Lowe, then in the Education Department (and later

Gladstone's Chancellor of the Exchequer), remarked acidly, 'We must educate our masters.' By the 1890s elementary education was compulsory. At the end of the century the school leaving-age was raised to twelve, in 1914 to fourteen, in 1947 to fifteen, and in 1972 to sixteen. At present only 15 per cent of fifteen-year-olds stay in full-time education —as opposed to, say, 45 per cent in the U.S.A. So universal education in England is a young growth. It was created with the public-school system as an ideal, with prefects, division into houses, and such similarities. More recently, comprehensive schools have begun to shake down into their own style, and the public schools no longer seem to be at the top of the system, but to be part of another system altogether. Teachers, educators and particularly children themselves have shown a healthy disrespect for the old pattern. And our parents are amazed how 'young people these days' can treat with such small respect the education it is such a privilege to receive.

My father left school at twelve. His first job was in a pawnshop. On Friday nights, when their husbands brought home the wages, the women came to redeem the family bedding. My father's job was to climb up to the loft and send the bundles down a chute into the shop. For such people hope of 'bettering themselves' lay in self-education. The Mechanics' Institutes, the university extension courses, the Workers' Educational Association, the University Correspondence College (at which H. G. Wells was a tutor): these were the organized expression of the spirit in which my father set out to teach himself the theory of engineering. In the bookcase at home there were about twenty ordinary books, most of them accidentally acquired, but also complete sets of *Home University Course*, *Harmsworth's Self-Educator*, *Harmsworth's Encyclopedia* and *Everywoman's Encyclopedia*.

For us, his children, bettering ourselves meant more than the acquisition of knowledge. At the age of ten, in that classically oriented prep school in Buckinghamshire, I learnt that it was not enough to be bright. That might have been sufficient for the masters, but the boys had stricter requirements. For my first term I was the school victim, legitimate prey for every form of nastiness. They mimicked my 'common' vowels. Between lessons I was made to say 'How now brown cow' again and again. In the dormitory after lights-out each boy in turn would describe what he least liked about me. Memories of idyllic picnics in the grounds with my parents on Speech Day—the cows grazing in the park beyond the ha-ha—are confused with other memories, when those old cedars, and the great dark yew hedges take on a nightmare aspect. I am hunted by yelling packs of boys; sobbing and terrified, I hide in the undergrowth, praying (actually calling on God) for the end of free time. Before the beginning of the second term I was panic-stricken at the idea of going back. But how could I explain to my parents what I was frightened of?

It is difficult, describing this sort of experience, not to seem to wallow in self-pity. I do not doubt that I had unfortunate habits. (One boy in that dormitory court-martial complained that I made too much noise with my heels on the wooden floor of the dining-room when it was my turn to wait at table: I know—and knew instinctively then—the irritating self-dramatization he meant.) But mostly what I was learning were the rules of class behaviour. The accent, the language ('lavatory' not 'toilet', 'How do you do?' not 'Pleased to meet you'), the manners (raise your cap, give up your seat, hold your knife *thus*). So class, like classics, was rules too, somehow confused with manners. And it is an impressionable time of life. I am still offended to see a woman smoking in the street, and I myself, if I were hungry, would hesitate to buy a bun or a chocolate bar to eat as I walked along the street.

These rules were what we went to school to learn. And with that teenage arrogance, we children, odious little *arrivistes*, brought them back and tried to impose them on our parents. Partly because of changing fashion, but also very much because of us, the meal that had always been 'tea', which we had soon after five thirty when my father came in from the yard, came to be known as 'supper'. The teapot disappeared from the table, and instead of bread and jam and cake after the first course, we began to have some sort of 'pudding'. More and more we sat in the drawing-room in the evenings, instead of saving it for special occasions. All the woodwork in the house was painted a gingerish brown, stippled, but that was repainted white throughout. With monumental tact I gave my father a decanter for his birth-day – 'That', I was saying, 'is what you put the sherry in.' In the garden we tore out 'the laurels' and replaced them with herbaceous beds. On special occasions, when we thought fit to go to the theatre, we tended to want to go to ballet at Covent Garden, and we all tried to appreciate it as best we could.

But what the knowledge of the rules – inaccurate and partial certainly – failed to give me was the necessary assur-ance. That was what I – then – so desperately craved. When I was eighteen my headmaster could still write, with the unsympathetic tone typical of school reports, 'Far too gauche for a boy in his position'.* Though I now wonder how such a report could help the condition, I knew what he meant: those agonizing lunches at the top table when he sat next to each prefect in rotation. I was always too self-conscious to think of anything to say. It never occurred to me to think that he should have put me at my ease, that *he* was far too gauche for a man in his position.

Still making use of those Latin idioms learnt by heart at the age of eleven, I got an exhibition – a sort of second-class scholarship – to Cambridge. At the age of fourteen I had

---

* Thomas Bewick, the engraver, said, a hundred and fifty years ago, of the upstart Newcastle farmers: 'They acted the gentleman very awkwardly, and could not, in these times, drink anything but wine.' My friend Jorrocks similarly declared, of champagne, that 'it gives one werry gentlemanly ideas.'

entered a dormant period that lasted fifteen years. So many
important experiences passed in a dream. I was passive,
living off the fat of earlier years. Even physically: at fourteen I had been one of the fastest sprinters in the school,
but I grew slower, not faster, as I got older. Cambridge
passed, three years of dutiful attendance at lectures, half-
hearted rugger, toasting buns by the gas fire, giving and at-
tending the most discreet sherry parties. And at a distance
admiring secretly the dashing few who found girl-friends
among the waitresses at The Coffee Pot, who got drunk,
illegally drove cars, were reporters on *Varsity*, appeared in
the Footlights review ... It has left me with a sense of wasted
time—and a slight embarrassment. When they all say,
'What a great time you must have had,' how can I answer,
'Well, actually, it was rather dull'?

As part of the Cambridge classics faculty, I was eligible
to take part in the triennial Greek play. For two weeks in the
Arts Theatre we performed Aeschylus' *Agamemnon* before
an audience of school parties of teenage girls. I had hoped
for some major dramatic part, but at the audition at King's
that fatal self-consciousness made my limbs wooden. The
producer was 'Dadie' Rylands. The name meant nothing to
me then, but now I know he had been a decoration of the
Bloomsbury set: 'the usual contingent of male "beauties",'
commented Strachey's friend Carrington, describing a party
in nautical costume, 'Douglas, Dadie, Angus and many
others, all in white ducks'. More than thirty years later he
was still hanging round Cambridge, exuding a somewhat
theatrical charm and an air of perpetual amusement. The
trouble was, I had the feeling he was laughing at me. And
some of the time he certainly was—but in the most direct,
open, sympathetic way. But that was a concept too sophisticated for my hesitant social sense. I ended up as one of the
chorus of old men.

For much of the play the chorus stood about on the stage
in blue nightshirts, trying to look old and wise behind their

whiskers, while Clytemnestra delivered her long venomous speeches. I only understood the gist of what she was saying. And she — the girl who played the part — was amazed at this ignorance. How could one not understand every word of the text? A Greek scholar ... ? A great gap opened, the sudden realization that this was what it meant to read classics: one understood Greek and Latin as one might French.

There were others who took part in the play, apart from the principals and us serious middlemen in the chorus: the walk-on men who played palace servants, local inhabitants, slaves to drag Agamemnon's chariot. Their attitude was very different. With predictable irreverence they called Clytemnestra 'Clitoris' (she heartily despised their casual ways). They sauntered on to the stage and looked round as if they were thinking of buying it. If an evening performance clashed with some social engagement, they simply arranged for a friend to take their place. 'Oh,' I overheard one giving instructions after a matinee, 'you don't have to *do* anything. You wander on here, flash your jack, and wander off with the others.'

One afternoon, while we old men, in our blue gowns and our heavy, itchy beards, stood at the front of the stage, shaking our heads and discussing in iambic pentameters the impending doom of the house of Atreus, I noticed from the corner of my eye that the man next me was shuffling away sideways. This was not a scheduled move. I turned slowly, in character I hoped, to see what was going on. His eyes — blue, I remember, in the heavily made-up face — were signalling some urgent message, as he shuffled into the wings. I guessed he must be ill. I moved to cover his retreat, casting about to remember if he had solo lines later in the scene.

Actually he was not ill. Standing at the end of our line of old men, his eye had been caught by a movement in the wings. He, too, turned casually. Two of the walk-ons were beckoning, signalling urgently. He feared his beard was falling off, or his underwear showing. He went closer. Still they beckoned. Then, when he was within reach, they caught the edge of his robe and began to pull. He resisted, attempting to retain the stance of an old man, turning a worried expression to the leader of the chorus while straining to keep his position. But gradually he had to give way, sliding, he hoped unobtrusively, from the stage. At his cue there was a long and dreadful silence until the next speaker had the sense to continue.

Yet afterwards, to my amazement, Dadie Rylands was quite unperturbed. 'That's all right,' he said when the walk-ons casually apologized — both he and they giving the impression that the apology, like raising your hat, satisfied some behavioural form that neither considered important — 'One year someone walked across the stage stark naked. For a bet.' He smiled conspiratorially. They'd have to do better than that to astonish *him*.

That is what these people had — assurance. It might not be the only requisite but it is a basic necessity for a gentleman. 'Five years in a luke-warm bath of snobbery,' George Orwell called that education. For me it merely changed some habits, in a more or less conscious shaping of a different style. It is difficult to understand, and somewhat embarrassing to recall, the naïve eagerness with which I copied my betters. Why, there was even a time, when, inspired by some aristocratic fellow-officer in the Royal Horse Artillery, I took to wearing my handkerchief tucked up my sleeve.

What do those prospective mothers-in-law mean, though, when they tell their friends that 'he's not quite a gentleman'? Mrs Sweetenham once told me that my father was 'one of Nature's gentlemen'. Mr Watts very recently referred to him as 'a real white man'. At the time I took Mrs Sweetenham's phrase as a compliment, as I believe my father might have done himself. I am sure she intended it kindly, but now it does seem to have an awfully patronizing sound.

Yet it is not necessarily ancestry that 'Mummy' wants. 'There is almost certainly no family in the land, from the

Queen's downward, whose complete ancestry can be tabulated for six or seven generations backward without coming on some forbears of no higher status than *innkeeper* or plumber,' (My italics.) We have this comforting information from the author of a biography of the Queen herself, Mr Dermot Morrah. Mummy knows this perfectly well, though she would rather forget it. Society has a conveniently short memory. But at least she would expect one generation in the professions. The son of a garage owner would be socially embarrassing. Even in 1971, Miss Lucy Keymer, of the Norland Nursery Training College, spoke of the girls she trains as nannies as 'jolly good types really. We have girls here from private, public, grammar and convent schools, daughters of professional people, farmers' daughters, and some people from very humble backgrounds. We even had one girl whose father was a garage proprietor.' Maybe — but my sister would certainly not have entertained the idea of being a nanny.

Mummy would also hope for a 'good' accent — public school at least, aristocratic/Oxford preferably ... Professor Alan Ross, Professor of Linguistics at Birmingham University, who has received a certain public recognition for his notation of class demarcations, says, 'It is solely by its language that the upper class is clearly marked off from the others.' * But clothes are important too. There is a required style, or lack of style: to wear a brown suit in the City can still ruin your chance of a partnership.

The whole world knows that the English are obsessed with class. It seems at times that the whole world is obsessed with the English obsession with class. 'This is an age', says the *Sunday Times*, 'in which the working class has come into

---

* In an article published in 1956, Professor Ross first suggested the classification 'U' (for 'Upper Class') and 'non-U'. Of course, it can be an amusing game: no *gentleman* would keep an Alsatian dog, show fear of horses, put milk first in his tea-cup, bother to clean his car. But equally, no gentleman would play such a game; true gentlemen are not concerned with the opinions of others. And Professor Ross's interest in the subject is itself, surely, rather common?

its own.' *New Society*, dispensing popular sociology, carries articles on 'Social Class and the Health Service' and similar matters. 'Income is the modern form of class.' 'People act in terms of status but talk about it in terms of class.' Class is moving, changing, but it sticks. It is doomed, but it is a long time dying. In some jobs la-di-dah talk is already an embarrassment. The process is actually reversed: some people deliberately de-posh their accent, preferring to keep down with the Atkinses. But that inversion is just as much a class consciousness. And the judgment is made on the outward style. Manners Makyth Englishman.

5. *The Posterior Shrine*

Women journey by widely different ways, but by whatever windings they may wander ... there is only one crown and common ground of all their differences—wickedness.

> Walter Map, Archdeacon of Oxford, 1197

'Get off. You've done it ... And your language is most revolting.'

> His wife, reported by Walter in *My Secret Life* (1888)

The curious work, *The Cries of London* ... shows us a little cane seller, running through the streets crying: Come buy my little Tartars, my pretty little Jemmies; no more than a halfpenny a piece.

> Guillaume Apollinaire (1880–1918), Introduction to French translation of *Fanny Hill*

No misfortune broke the even tenor of his life, except the loss of his two wives.

> John Buchan of Sir Henry Cromwell, 1934

It is difficult to avoid the conclusion that British men and women traditionally fear one another because of some sexual tension. Or at least that British men fear British women, and that the history of their attitudes is the history of successive attempts to avoid the frightening alternative of having to treat them as equal and intelligent humans. Like colonial natives, women are dangerous if not kept down. Their threat can be neutralized in various ways, from physical force to a patronizing pretence of equality.

The Christian Church has always had difficulty with women, but that is mainly the fault of its obsession with sex as sin. Pre-Christian Britain was openly carnal. Encountering this, the Church was shocked. In the eighth century, St Boniface, a Benedictine missionary from Devon, declared that his countrymen 'utterly despise matrimony ... and continue to live in lechery and adultery after the manner of neighing horses and braying asses'. The English scholar Alcuin agreed: 'The land has been absolutely submerged under a flood of fornication, adultery and incest, so that the very semblance of modesty is entirely absent.' In Arthurian England, and well into the Middle Ages, the Church fought vainly to sublimate the forthright earthiness of British lust. Trial marriages, affairs, illegitimacy and open animality were the normal state. Indeed, up until the Reformation, in Scotland trial marriage was a normal arrangement. Small wonder the Church was obsessed with sex. It seemed everyone else was.

'Woman tempted me,' Man can say to excuse his own indulgence. This was the medieval view. 'A Good Woman is but like an eel put in a bagge amongst five hundered snakes, and if a man shall have the luck to grope out that one Eel from all the snakes, yet he hath at best a wet eel by the tail.' The British view was crystallizing: a woman is an inferior creature, a necessary nuisance, naturally tainted, but nevertheless not to be taken seriously by sensible men. The medieval lord considered it beneath him to be jealous of the troubadours and sighing lovers who paid court to his wife, just as a modern business-lord ignores those hairdressers and interior decorators who hang round rich women.

Under the Church's guidance Eve became the 'mother of perdition', the eternal temptress estranging man from God. In the old wedding ceremony the wife promised to be 'bonny and buxom in bed and at board'; now she promised to 'love, honour and obey'. Fighting their own lustful imaginings, churchmen grew increasingly hysterical. John Knox, the Scottish Presbyterian, seeming to feel the danger that men might slip back in the eternal battle, was moved to the most intense attacks. With magnificent tactlessness, he published the first (of six) *Blast of the Trumpet against the Monstrous Regiment of Women* just at the time of Elizabeth I's accession. ('Regiment' in this case meant 'authority'. The Queen was understandably offended.) Knox himself had a somewhat complicated life with various women. The contemplation of female domination drove him to extreme language: 'Whosoever receiveth from a woman office or authority are adulterous and bastard officers before God ... Nature, I say, doth paint [women] further to be weak, frail, impatient, feeble and foolish;* and experience hath

---

* Elizabeth seems to be answering this very accusation in her famous Armada speech: 'I know I have the body of a weak and feeble woman, but I have the heart and stomach of a king, and a king of England too.' Victoria, on the other hand, more feminine than Elizabeth, separated the conception of herself as monarch from the recognition of herself as a woman. To Theodore Martin, official biographer of the Prince Consort (in five volumes) and a lifelong friend, she confided almost girlishly, 'The Queen is most anxious to enlist everyone who can speak or write to join in checking this mad, wicked folly of "Women's Rights", *with all its attendant horrors,* on which her poor feeble sex is bent, forgetting every sense of womanly feeling and

declared them to be inconstant, variable, cruel, and lacking the spirit of counsel and regiment.'

There is another thread that runs through English sexual life—doubtless connected with this fear of matriarchy, of Britannia actually coming to rule—and that is a backside fixation. The connection between 'swishing' and sexual stimulation may be universal, but not for nothing is flagellation *le vice anglais*: as a nation we specialize in this part of the anatomy. 'Nothing is more ordinary in England', the Duchess of Orléans wrote in 1698, 'than this unnatural vice.' Anglo-Saxons are anyway inclined to be pear-shaped—an advantage the wasp waist and the bustle were designed to emphasize. And seaside postcards to ridicule: leaning on the harbour wall, like fat babies grotesquely enlarged, presenting their mountainous posteriors, holidaymakers are 'Waiting for the Smacks'. The word 'bum' can still raise a giggle. Sexually we are a nation of adolescents.

En France on mange bien : en Angleterre, on chie bien. Puritan toilet training recurs later in life, like a shock-wave, in lavatory humour. At school, when we were translating Aristophanes once with 'Crack' (here and there skipping an embarrassing couplet), he positioned himself at the back of the class so that we, obediently facing front, could not see his face, and he said in a tone of great bravado, 'There's a perfectly good Anglo-Saxon word for this ... arse.' * Even in the Army, when I was an officer cadet, the most important advice our training officer, Major Singleton, could give us

---

propriety ... It is a subject which makes the Queen so furious that she cannot contain herself. Woman would become the most hateful, heartless and disgusting of human beings were she allowed to unsex herself; and where would be the protection that man was intended to give to the weaker sex?'

* This pronunciation was recently quite common also for the word 'ass': 'You silly arse', my father would say. It accounts for the Victorian story of the boy in school who forgot how Samson killed the Philistines: his friend whispered the answer, 'Jawbone of an ass', and the boy answered the teacher brightly, 'Jobbed them in the arse, sir.' That's a really English joke, a typically tortuous pun, with anal interest. American influence is substituting 'ass' for 'arse' in the English language.

—at least, the advice he most frequently repeated—was to 'make sure every morning you have a damn good rear.' And he was merely echoing Lord Baden-Powell, in whose *Scouting for Boys* the advice is given in almost the exact same words.

'Dear God, what have we here? A prodigy? That pleasure should come from pain, sweet from bitter, lust from bloody wounds? Does the same road lead to torment and delight?' (*Rare Verities: the Cabinet of Venus Unlocked*, Giovanni Sinibaldi, London 1658). Apparently for many Englishmen torment and delight are thus connected. At least one of our monarchs, Charles II, is said to have taken pleasure in this way. Under him, the cynical Restoration dramatists were at work. In *The Virtuoso* Thomas Shadwell has a character asking for flagellation, a taste he acquired, he says, at Westminster School. Flogging and beating were employed to correct everyone from infants to mutineers. Appreciatively Dr Johnson claimed, 'My master whipt me very well.' There seems indeed to have been a tradition of flogging headmasters, starting with Dr Colet at Eton and continuing at Westminster in the seventeenth century with Dr Busby (who presumably awoke Shadwell to its sexual possibilities), Dr Bowyer at Christ's Hospital, Dr Gill at St Paul's, Drs Drury and Vaughan at Harrow, Drs Keate, May and Edgeworth at Eton. The tradition has its own macabre humour: Dr Keate is said once to have confused the lists and flogged fifty Confirmation candidates. Swinburne, himself at Eton in the nineteenth century, celebrated his taste for the birch in the long poem *The Whippingham Papers*. Specialist brothels were set up in London, and their proprietors achieved a certain fame: George IV, never afraid of a scandal, visited Mrs Colet's establishment, and Mrs Teresa Berkley, whose establishment boasted her famous invention, the Berkley Horse, supposedly first put into practice in 1828, is said to have made ten thousand pounds in eight years and retired in comfort.

And indeed, when the floodgates of Victorian pornography opened, an amazing amount of what flowed through was flagellation fantasy, mostly of a ritual formality — written by 'Birchmaster', the rod wielded by Lady Termagant Flaybum, the stepmother of the erring boy who pleads (hopefully, and certainly in vain) for mercy. ' "Is it possible', said Mrs Trimmer, pulling his breeches down to his heels, 'that your mistress suffered this tyrannical gentleman to insult her in the manner she has represented?" ' 'What a treat in this seminary for idolators of the posterior shrine!' Who but an Englishman, and a Victorian clergyman at that — Dr Francis Kilvert — would describe a little girl, viewed from underneath a swing at a fair, as 'plump and smooth and in excellent whipping condition'?

Ritual school beating and nursery discipline might originally have been privileged experience, but now they are the common matter of sex literature.* Most (90 per cent, says Gillian Freeman on the basis of research in 1967) pornography available in England is flagellation and sado-masochistic — either pseudo-history (*The Kiss of the Whip*, *The History of Flagellation Practices*), or straight arousal (*My Naughty Wife*). In 'Personal Advertisement' magazines, about 50 per cent of *all* ads are for some sort of·C.P. (corporal punishment) or 'bondage', and school canes and 'leather spanking paddles' are offered for sale. And the majority of girls who offer service by advertisement (obviously 'straight' sex does not require the use of these channels) hint cutely at similar activities: 'Coloured governess', 'Stocks and bonds for sale', 'Miss Stern', 'Girl seeks driving post' ...

I can remember not even the slightest thrill from being beaten at school. I faced the prospect of physical pain with simple terror. Indeed in my case I believe it was an effective

---

* Though not all agree it should be. In a House of Lords debate, in 1971, Lord Clifford of Chudleigh said, 'I am worried about the effect of pornography on the lower-I.Q. members of the population. The educated people can cope with these things.' His own schooling seems to have failed to teach him to distinguish between I.Q. and education.

deterrent (that is not to say it was the right sort of effective deterrent) and I managed to avoid it except for about
half a dozen times. Nor did we ever hear of beating giving
pleasure, to either side. As prefects we were earnest and responsible, the self-conscious, post-war generation. You can
make it sound like *Tom Brown's Schooldays* by selecting the
right tales, and we did have the power to beat other boys for
some offences; but we were very serious about the responsibility of doing so. We still, however, did not reject the
system under which beating was expected. It did not occur
to us to question it. And indeed, as my brother and I reached
our teens, my mother, finding her natural force insufficient,
and that we were not cowed by the threat to 'tell your father
when he comes in', armed herself with a little whippy cane
that she kept on the picture-rail in the back hall above the
coats. I am not sure how she intended to use it—any sort of
ritual punishment would have been quite out of character
for our family. I can only recall being pursued tearfully
round the dining-room table—what for? Throwing a
wooden table-mat at my brother, I believe.

I have never at any time in my life had any sex instruction.
At my prep school it was well known that at the end of their
last term, boys were given a rather vague lecture warning
them of the sexual 'dangers' of public-school life. It might
have surprised Mr Evans to know that the contents of this
talk were common knowledge among those sexually obsessed little boys. The names of school-leavers were read out
in the chapel, where we had daily prayers and practised 'Oh
for the Wings of a Dove'. That term my name was read out
alone. I never had the lecture. Perhaps Mr Evans was embarrassed to give it *tête à tête*. Perhaps he thought I knew it
all already. Perhaps the lecture was a myth anyway. Indeed,
from the age of ten, sex had been a much-discussed topic.
And much practised. Those boys who could achieve results
proudly did so; others who could not determinedly went on
trying. In the dormitory after lights-out I discovered a

talent for story-telling and in a whisper I would tell hopefully pornographic tales. They were, I know now, rather
wildly inaccurate about the facts of sex.

That might have been corrected at the next school by the
information we were said to be given by our headmaster.
Again, the fact of this sex instruction was well known – but
the boys of my term never received the delicious summons.
I did once, however, in the holidays, see my housemaster
coming out of a shop in Soho that displayed books on sex
instruction – but that was later, when I had already bought
one for myself. ('Nudity is natural,' it said – I remember
this sentence clearly, not for the information, but for the
sudden vision it gave me of the author rationalizing his own
tastes – 'but some men have the harmless "perversion" of
preferring their wives to keep on their stockings.')

My father never told me anything either that might be
called the facts of life. When I was eighteen and just leaving
for the Army, he did find the opportunity to have a few words
with me. He wanted me to know that I could always come
to him for help if I got into trouble – and not just money, he
wanted to make that clear. Women I guessed was what was
on his mind, and I was touched that he who found it so hard
to talk of such things, and was anyway a silent man, should
have made such an effort. Of course I did not actually need
a sex lecture, but it might have been a healthier atmosphere
at home if the subject had not been totally taboo. And I am
well aware that some psychologists say that writers (and
others – doctors and explorers too) choose their profession
as a result of the frustrated search in youth for sexual knowledge.

At that prep school, where most boys started at the age of
eight, I had arrived a couple of years late. There was a Boy
Scout Troop, and a Cub Pack for the under-elevens. I was
eager to join, but it was not considered worth my being a
Cub for the short while before Scout age. Finally I joined
Woodpecker Patrol, known as 'Peckers', in great excitement.

There was a Scout loft above the old stables in the courtyard of the school; but more important were the camp kitchens. Here and there in the grounds of the school, hidden among the shrubs and trees, each Troop had a small area, a 'kitchen', with a floor of bare packed earth, a fireplace, with a wooden tripod for the cooking-pot, a covered store, a seat made from a log for every person. In those sacred groves each Troop occupied itself learning knots or lashing ropes, signalling in morse or semaphore, and other such practical matters. *

But once a year in the summer term the older scouts went on a camping weekend. Harnessed to the Scout cart, we dragged the tents, food and cooking equipment a mile along the road to a remote field. Our Scoutmaster was an ex-Army major who had served in India. To me he seemed old, and since it was wartime he must presumably have been too old for military service, but his manner was hearty, his bearing upright, his moustache bristling.

We were all men together — one man and a dozen boys — so clothing was not really necessary out there in the camp. When Miss Lee walked across the fields to visit us on Sunday afternoon we wrapped ourselves in towels and brewed tea for her in the cooking-pot (Army style, thick and sweet with condensed milk). The boys occupied the large circular tent, feet to the middle like the petals of a flower. Our Scoutmaster slept separately in a small tent. He had brought his gun with him to shoot rabbits for the pot. He planned to set out soon after dawn on Sunday, when the rabbits would be feeding undisturbed, and he offered to take one boy with him. Of course we all clamoured to go, but he would not trust more than one of us not to disturb the rabbits. The un-

* Boy Scouts were founded in 1907 by Major-General Baden-Powell, and based on his experience in training recruits in the Indian Army, and a cadet force of boys during the siege of Mafeking — from which Baden-Powell emerged a national hero. Scouting is inspired by a spirit of self-conscious imperialism — actually hoping to 'see ourselves as others see us' — and simple resourcefulness. One in six British men have been Scouts at one time in their lives.

lucky ones were deeply disappointed. Before we were awake
the next morning he and the chosen boy had set out for
their expedition. They too, we learned, at the master's sug-
gestion, set out wearing towels only. And these they discarded at the first gatepost, and stalked on without, crawling
naked, Indian file through the dewy grass. It sounded like
an adventure, and we all wished we had gone. They were
back with a dead rabbit before the rest of us were up, scam-
pering out to the latrines with bare feet, trying to avoid the
great pale slugs that came out of the hay stubble.

That day the rabbit was to be our dinner. We cooked it
with potatoes and onions in a stew over the fire. While it
was cooking, our Scoutmaster gave us a challenge: he bet
us that, if we tied him up, he would escape; and if he could
not, he would eat his stew like that, like a dog from a dish.
Under his instructions we tied his arms behind his back,
and his legs together. And it seemed we did it so well that
he lost his bet. He writhed and twisted, but he could not
escape. We were delighted. It had never happened before,
he said; he had *always* escaped when other camps had tied
him up. Well, it was no good; he would keep his side of the
bargain. A plate of stew was put in front of him on the
ground, and he lay uncomfortably on his stomach, hands
tied behind him, and slobbered the food from the plate. It
made an awful mess of his moustache.

Now, after meals we rinsed our plates in the stream near
the site, scrambling down the steep bank. It must have been
a dry spell, because I remember the bank was hard rough
mud — perhaps churned up by cattle coming down to drink.
The Scoutmaster, who had got rather messy over his meal
— he was just wearing a pair of football shorts — suggested
that while we were at it we should give him a dip in the
stream. He promised that if we untied his legs he would not
run away. So someone — I think it was the boy who went
shooting with him — undid the rope from his legs and led
him to the top of the bank. 'I'm not going to go in by

myself,' the major said. 'You'll have to push me in. And' —
indicating the shorts — 'you'll have to take these off. I don't
want to get them wet.' So someone did — I think it was the
same boy — and the master sort of lay down and rolled down
the rough bank into the stream. That is my most vivid
memory of Scouting days.

A backside fixation and homosexuality might seem to be
connected. But I know of no evidence that the British are
more inclined to homosexual practice than other nations.
We certainly view it with less tolerance than some, but it is
also true that, apart from those we can label and dispose of
easily as 'eccentrics', we are generally intolerant of deviation.
It is a subject of universal fascination, the cause of much
whispering and speculative gossip. The naval tradition
(rum, sodomy, prayers and the lash, according to Churchill;
the rum ration and flogging are both now discontinued),
church choirs, public schools, Boy Scout Troops, universi-
ties, the theatre, the Guards Regiments, left-wing intellectuals (the intellectual fraternity of the 'twenties that included
such people as J. M. Keynes, E. M. Forster and Lytton
Strachey, was known, says Professor Noel Annan, as 'the
Homintern') — ordinary people often write off such exclusive groups by peopling them with 'nancy boys'. Recently,
on top of a bus in Fleet Street, I overheard an American
visitor, as the dome of St Paul's came into view, tell his
English host that he had visited Cambridge, and how he
had admired King's College Chapel. 'Ah yes,' said the
Englishman. 'It's strange, you know. King's and Trinity,
those wonderful chapels — and they don't believe in God.
They're run by homosexuals.'

The sexual repression of public-school education is also
frequently quoted as the cause for widespread British effem-
inacy. Logic hardly supports this view. In the first place,
only three in a hundred boys go to public schools. Second,
if you accept that sexual proclivities are formed at the infant
stage, though you might pick up some homosexual habits in

a community without girls, to continue to practise them when no longer necessary only indicates that habits are not easily broken.

This is such a well-known British subject that I hesitate to add my own evidence. Generations of public-school boys have reported sodomy and gained a happily scandalized audience. Briefly: at my school there certainly was sexual activity. I believe that the extent was in a way fashionable, depending more than anything—as did beating—on the attitude of senior boys in each house. Boys of eighteen are young men; boys of thirteen can be winsome as girls— 'smooths' indeed. A few of them took advantage of this and, playing a female role, deliberately seduced older boys. In other cases, older boys pursued younger as they would girls, and if successful, used them in the same way. But I should guess that the activity was—to make it decent with Latin—more intercrural than anal.

The whole house slept in one dormitory, fifty beds in a long hall divided into stalls by waist-high partitions. You started at one end as a new boy, and moved up each term. In the dark, boys from the senior end might visit boys at the junior end. It was a furtive traffic, betrayed by creaking boards and springs. There were no open romantic friendships, none of the famous flamboyant attachments between games captains and pretty little fags. There is no doubt of the sexual interest of being waited on by sweet boys, or entertaining them to tea in your study, but if the attraction was openly admitted, the activity rarely was. It is impossible to quantify such a secret trade. I can only give my own experience: I was 'visited' about five times in two years, until I gathered the courage to refuse; I never myself, as a senior boy, made such an expedition. Perhaps the practice never would be blatant. Rupert Brooke, temporarily acting as a housemaster at Rugby, after his father's death in that position, said, 'What is the whole duty of a housemaster? To prepare boys for Confirmation, and turn a blind eye on sodomy.' Perhaps we English need to feel guilty about sex. But partly at least it was the fact that people show you what you want to see, and I disapproved. As a senior boy I was serious and rather prim, awfully responsible. I think I regret that now: at an age of high animal vitality, why deny a natural source of pleasure, fighting sexuality with daily exercise and the morning cold bath?* Girls would be best, but as the sailor says in *Fanny Hill*, 'any port in a storm'.

However, the dearth of girls – and it was no better in the holidays, for me and I guess many others, being at a distance from school-friends and without local friends – no doubt retarded the beginning of sexual experience. One year a party of boys from school toured Holland with the school production of *Hamlet*. Most of us were bewildered by these sophisticated, co-educational, sexually experienced Dutch children. They spoke to us frankly about sex, assuming common attitudes, like fellow-countrymen met abroad (we were fellow-countrymen in the private state of youth, the universal conspiracy). But we were embarrassed. The girls thought we were peculiar – perhaps those stories about English public-school boys *were* true ...

Well, only partly true. What most of us were was *scared* of women. We were afraid of the unfamiliar. We had been brought up to think of them as a different race. Their nakedness and ours were segregated secrets – apartheid of the sexes. Dedicated to a doctrine of continence, the removal of girls must have seemed to our elders the logical first step. The tablets of public-school law were engraved in the nineteenth century. The famous Dr Arnold, appointed headmaster of Rugby in 1828, declared, 'My object will be, if possible, to form Christian men, for Christian boys I can

* A dip in a bath filled with cold water, designed to banish luxurious thoughts inspired by waking in a warm bed. There were two bath-tubs between fifty boys, and the hot-bath rota allowed two twenty-minute baths a week. But there was a strange bath-house ritual when, every afternoon after games, the junior boys stood at the handbasins and scooped hot water over themselves with tin mugs; the seniors sat on benches at footbaths and did the same, and the prefects jammed three or four each, feet over the side, in the two baths.

scarcely hope to make.' 'One of the noblest objects in the world in these our days,' said William Acton in 1857, advising on the training of boys ' — a *continent* man.' He defines continence: 'the voluntary and entire forbearance from sexual excitement or indulgence in any form'. * A hopeless and unnatural purpose, it may not have perverted the sexual drives, but it did fatally poison the attitudes of those boys to the opposite sex.

To divide women into two categories, saints and prostitutes, is to insult both groups; but that is what Englishmen have attempted to do. We have told one group that for them an awareness of sexual pleasure is a vulgar and evil fault; we have turned to the other for our own sexual pleasure, and despised them for agreeing to participate. It is a typical flowering of the British hypocrisy. It reached its height in the famous Victorian sexual charade; but the legacy of those sickening decades are with us still, subtly influencing national attitudes.

The character of Victorianism was a sort of vulgar prudery. Perhaps unfairly I see it made flesh in the sight of the Queen herself, rather overweight, watering her Scotch with claret; yet her ministers feared to offend her delicacy — the story goes — by putting before her a Bill dealing with the legality of anal intercourse. The morals of this peculiar age were derived from the evangelist revival of Puritanism at the end of the eighteenth century. Utility was the measure of everything, according to Jeremy Bentham (1748–1832) and the Benthamites. Every institution had to withstand a simple test: What's the use of it?

This was the great age of *property*, when the swiftly growing law of Torts — by which the remedy for a civil wrong lies in an action for damages — extended the conception of property by putting a *financial* value on defamation,

---

* Masturbation, Acton had earlier pronounced — with the authority of a leading expert on sexual disorders — gave rise to hysteria, asthma, epilepsy, melancholia, mania, suicide, dementia and general paralysis of the insane.

seduction (value, that is, to the master or the husband of the seduced), negligence, fraud, 'nuisance'. *Possessions* are nine-tenths of the law. So the importance of property entered even the bedroom. It was an offence against property to employ a woman's body without paying for it: the adulterer takes something that the husband is paying for, the seducer something that the father is paying for. The women themselves were not consulted; they were merely flesh. Until 1843, indeed, women and children were working under-ground with less dignity than beasts of burden.

'Married life', explained the *Saturday Review* in 1857, 'is women's profession; and to this life her training—that of dependence—is modelled. Of course, by not getting a hus-band, or losing him, she may find that she is without resources. All that can be said of her is, she has failed in business and no social reform can prevent such failures.' Keeping women in that position of dependence pervaded the attitudes of the time. Mary Wollstonecraft, a pioneer of emancipation, published *A Vindication of the Rights of Women* in 1792: Horace Walpole hysterically declared her 'a hyena in petticoats'. Four years later William Acton de-clared that 'it is a vile aspersion' to say that women are capable of sexual feeling. John Stuart Mill called for the 'morality of justice' for women, but Gladstone agreed with the Queen that women's suffrage would be dangerous and unnatural—'a trespass', he said, 'upon the delicacy, the purity, the refinement, the elevation of her own nature, which are the present sources of its power.' The ladies themselves, successively indoctrinated, saw education as the 'doom of maidenhood'.

In the Victorian family the children were educated in the repressive virtues: piety, tolerance, good faith, self-reliance, industry and a perverted version of tolerance. The master of the house (the phrase, still common in a slightly jocular version, is significant) was permitted escape from the in-tolerable atmosphere of the 'sanctity of the home', but on his return he discarded his unfortunate masculine sexuality with his ulster in the hall. His wife certainly should not expect any ardour from him as a right: 'No nervous or feeble young man', the same Acton declares, 'need, therefore, be deterred from marriage by any exaggerated notion of the arduous duties required of him.' And, 'a newly married man ... need not fear that his wife will require the excitement or in any respect imitate the ways of a courtesan.'

With the prudery, the vulgarity: the courtesan and the wife both necessary participants in the accepted pattern of life. This necessitated a sort of open duplicity. Lord Palmerston, trying to persuade the Turks of the impropriety of polygamy, was met with the reply: 'Ah, my lord, we'll do what you do — we'll show one in public, and hide the others.' A lady was expected to possess a blind eye. She turned it as she passed down Regent Street: the sunny side had been taken over entirely by streetwalkers. The Haymarket was worse, crowded with girls in 'black satin and rouge', and many of the coffee-shops advertised 'beds' in their windows. Nelson-like she applied her blind eye to the spyglass when men took to sea-bathing (until the 'seventies men bathed, in separate areas but in view of spectators, without costumes). Even to *The Times* she was intermittently blind: reflecting the common assumption that it was 'a man's world', it reported scandalous cases ('It has been our disagreeable duty to publish evidence of a very disgusting character,' it sighed in 1862) and printed naughty letters, because women did not read it. 'Ask no questions and you'll be told no lies', a rebuke from my childhood, describes the position of these women.

The pretence was so shallow that it could only be kept up by the women tacitly agreeing not to ask awkward questions. So they did not ask specifically about the activity in the Haymarket, or what men talked of after dinner when the ladies retired to the drawing-room (dirty stories of the 'other life', sexual tips and news of the latest 'Dancing Rooms'), or the precise timetable of their visits to their clubs ('a male virgin was regarded in the smoking-room as a rather poor-spirited fellow'), * or the profession of the 'pretty horse-breakers', the dashingly dressed girls who held court at the reins of their elegant ponies in Rotten Row. 'Can any scene in the world', asked George Augustus Sala the journalist in 1859, 'equal Rotten Row at four in the afternoon and in the full tide of the season?' (May to mid-July). What made it so extraordinary were those horsebreakers, the fashionable ladies of the town. 'Who drives the most rampageous ponies?' — this in a letter to *The Times* — 'Who do all the best girls ape in dress and deportment and equipage if they can; aye and in talk too? Who first set the fashion of the "pork-pie" hat?' The answer is Skittles, who claimed, with some justification (having the Crown Prince as a patron) to be as much queen of the alternative world as Victoria was of the world of appearances. Sir Edwin Landseer, the master of portentous Victorian painting, hung his portrait of her in the Royal Academy exhibition, archly claiming it to be a portrait of a 'Miss Gilbert'. No one, not even the respectable ladies who asked no questions, was for a minute deceived.

'Regard for the proprieties of life scarcely remains,' reported *London Society*. 'It is no uncommon thing for a young man to appear in the Park escorting a "celebrity" of this kind, and as he passes some lady of his acquaintance, to lift his hat in courteous recognition of her, as though there was nothing to be ashamed of in his companion.' Shame was certainly at a premium. It was simply unnecessary. Men had proprietary rights, permanent or temporary, over all four categories — servants, dependent relatives, wives and 'gay' ladies — and shame did not enter into that relationship. Women were paid to possess a blind eye when required. The Queen might be morally severe, but her Prime

* After a dinner with Dickens and Carlyle, Emerson wrote in his diary: 'Dickens replied that incontinence is so much the rule in England that if his own son was particularly chaste he should be alarmed on his account, as if he could not be in good health.'

Minister for ten years, 'Cupid' Palmerston, as she well knew
—he was caught in the corridors of Windsor Castle making
for the bedroom of a lady-in-waiting—was a genuine
old Regency rake, a notorious satyr, cited as co-respondent
at the age of seventy-nine,* tottering into old age with
his breeches round his ankles. Even in politicians irregular
sexual relationships were socially accepted. The villas of
St John's Wood and Regent's Park were occupied by the
mistresses of prominent men. Henry Dupré Labouchère,
the founder and editor of *Truth* (a paper founded in 1876),
lived openly with an actress, Henrietta Hodson. At campaign meetings hecklers got in the way of shouting, ' 'ow's
'enrietta 'enry?' So Labouchère began his speech one evening thus: 'I wish to convey to you all the gratifying
intelligence that Henrietta is quite well.' That arch use of
high-flown language—a very English scene.

The vitality of that alternative Victorian world, partly
mythologized in the distorting rear-view mirror of history,
was nevertheless quite different from the present situation,
where prostitutes (and indeed 'mistresses') cater only for the
middle-aged and the unattractive. It has become a far more
furtive trade. The Victorian double-vision, sensitive to the
point that trousers, being in contact with men's lower limbs,
could only be referred to as 'inexpressibles', yet allowed
women openly to contemplate men bathing naked—the
taboo of course was verbal: much that was obvious was all
the same 'unmentionable', because of that male dominance.
It is that verbal taboo that supports dirty stories. And it is
not just in the sexual area: there are a lot of things the English would rather not talk about.

Unsupported by the defiant, confident class of males,
prostitution becomes more furtive as society becomes more
permissive—reverting to a prostitute is now a new kind of
shame. Until 1959 London prostitutes were streetwalkers in

* Hoist by his own petard: Palmerston had himself forced through parliament a
law by which divorce was brought within the scope of the civil courts.

the literal sense. At the time I was lodging in a house in Shepherd Market, in Mayfair. We used to watch the girls from our windows. Hopefully they would wriggle as a man approached: 'Hello, darling. Like to have a lovely time?' (The Victorian version of this proposal, with exquisite verbal propriety, was, 'Are you good-natured, dear?') Next us was a house whose curtains were never drawn back, except on the ground floor, where a neon sign in the window—it is still there—advertised simply 'Private Tuition in French'.* At two o'clock in the morning, when work was over, the girls gathered in the kitchen. Often they made rather a noise and, somewhat diffidently, we asked if they could tone it down. With many apologies, they said they certainly would. You see, in our streets, they were a nice type of girl —many of them more the maternal sort—who would not presume to speak to locals they recognized while other people were about, but at quiet times, when you came home late, would say goodnight or pass a few words about the weather. Of course it is evident they all had hearts of gold.

The law now, since 1959, is that it is 'an offence for a common prostitute to loiter or solicit in a street or public place for the purpose of prostitution'. The men who seek such company are free to accost every woman in the street without legal liability. Outside London cars have become the commonest sexual rendezvous. In London lighted bell-pushes advertise 'Young French model—Walk Up' (French naturally); or cards outside stationers advertise in crude code 'Lost: ring inscribed "I love Dick" '. Businessmen's call-girls have no doubt always existed, and always will:

---

* To an Englishman the word 'French' is sufficient information. The legend of naughty Paris still persists. In pubs people nudge and wink and exclaim 'Ooh la la', and 'Gay Paree'—though Paris is now far primmer than London. But it was to Paris that Englishmen most easily travelled, and one of the reasons for doing so was to escape domestic restraint. To the Parisians the English appeared obsessed with sex, and very often perverted. The more irregular your sexual inclination, of course, the more likely you are to feel freer to practise it abroad. French hotels are 'understanding', we all know that. Underwear is advertised as French. French perfume, French kisses, French letters—'they order these things better in France.'

they are a sexual bonus and no part of sexual necessaries. As the social use of areas changes, so do the markets of flesh. The Victorian villas of St John's Wood are now the height of middle-class propriety; in the Haymarket the tarts have given place to flocks of young summer migrants from the United States. Years ago I have heard men say, contemptuously, 'like a Jermyn Street tart', but Jermyn Street as long as I have known it has been innocent of such trade. Just before the Street Offences Act, parts of Mayfair, Soho and the north side of Hyde Park were favourite beats. (Oddly, the bushes nearest Park Lane remained the scene of such transactions for at least a hundred years. Just before the Act I would sometimes walk there at night and observe this amazing traffic.) Now Soho, Paddington and Bayswater are the habitats of the London whore.

I hopefully imagine (and what little research there is supports this view*) that boys no longer need to go to prostitutes for their first experience. In a much more sexually open atmosphere, there is no need any longer for the man to claim the superiority of previous experience. But we did. I am talking now about 1950, and that was twenty years ago. But we are less than forty still, and that's the timescale on which we must measure social change. Shortly before I left school for National Service, a friend (and fellow prefect), a particularly ribald fellow – who, I guessed from his innuendoes, intermittently visited the junior end of the dormitory – went to Paris on his summer holiday. There, in a side-street off the top of the Champs-Elysées, after building his courage with quantities of wine, he picked up a prostitute, an imposing figure, generously built and expensively dressed in a fur-collared coat. She took him to her room, bade him wash himself. He was too drunk, so she did it for him, with almost disastrous results. He collapsed on the bed, excited

* M. Schofield, *The Sexual Behaviour of Young People* (1965), for instance. Paul Goodman, the American sociologist, making comparison with American youth, says of the English, 'Not least, in their oddly undemonstrative way, they seem to have more sexual security.'

but incapable of taking the initiative. She positioned her-self astride him and — it was all over. A fantastic experience, he said it was. But I suspect it left much to be desired. In-deed, robbed of a certain *French* glamour and translated to Soho, it might actually have been sordid.

To get sex with any girl other than a professional was to embark on a campaign of battle. It assumed the girl to be an adversary, needing to be won over by a trick, force, dope, drink or declarations of undying spiritual love. There was no doubt: she was bound to resist. Even if sexually inclined (and therefore suspect), she would think she ought not to do it. If she did do it, she'd take care to do it with anyone but the man she wanted to 'catch' and marry. 'All's fair in love and war' — because love *is* war. No wonder we boys felt such freaks with those uninhibited Dutch co-eds.

By the time I was conscripted for National Service, at eighteen, virginity was a burden that grew daily more op-pressive, threatening, it seemed, eventually to incapacitate me altogether. But circumstances did not provide much opportunity. A brief tour in Germany was spent on a pro-longed exercise. Most of the time I was in a state of nervous exhaustion and thinly disguised terror. Sexual problems took a second place.

After that I spent a year or so in Egypt on the shores of the Great Bitter Lake. Every town was out of bounds, ex-cept the main street of Ismailia during high daylight. No trips to Port Said, Alexandria, Cairo. At the edge of the desert we sat like an army of occupation. The Sweet Water Canal irrigated fields of carefully husbanded mud, and the Garrison polo ground, visited on quiet days by hoopoes and small white egrets, was a dazzling green: but our camp was out in the sand, where the only vegetation was the garden of the Officers' Mess. A mile to the west, the barren, rock cliff — known as 'the Escarpment' — seemed like the retaining wall of the endless rocky canyons of the desert.

A few of the officers had their wives with them, but as 'the situation deteriorated' (that is to say, the Egyptians stepped up their guerrilla activity in an effort to get us to leave), even they were sent home. At GHQ there were a few secretaries of a rather superior type, sent out from England. All their free time was spent as guests at the Officers' Club in Fayid with dashing captains from the Coldstream Guards. In the sex war, the rules of battle are reversed and inferiority of numbers is the great advantage. Those girls knew their power. For those of us not rich, handsome and commissioned in the Coldstream (these were not alternatives: all were necessary against that competition) sex was out of the question. In a camp of several hundred men there were two NAAFI ('Naffy': Navy, Army and Air Force Institutes) girls. And anyway, though it seems absurd now, it was out of the question for an officer to fraternize with that sort of girl (the GHQ secretaries came from homes where they had learnt to speak nicely and drink soup from the *side* of the spoon, tipping the plate *away* from them at the table). The NAAFI compound was heavily fortified with barbed-wire, and the girls served the canteen through a hatch small enough to keep them quite safe from marauding hands. Even so, they frequently complained that the men made unsavoury requests; they didn't understand that the whole regiment was affected by the pressure of unsatisfied lust.

The commanding officer, in the British tradition, decided that exercise and activity would disperse these dangerous accumulations. He declared that any officer who did not spend at least an hour a day on his military textbooks was unworthy of the Queen's commission. That could hardly be expected to apply to us conscripts, but even the regulars spent the hot afternoon hours in their tents lying on their beds with the latest books, banned in Britain and imported from America to the English bookshop.*

---

* *The Body's Rapture*, I recall, was then considered dangerously hot stuff: a protracted, lyrical and supremely tasteful progress through five hundred pages to the wedding night of a perfect spiritual love.

Two or three evenings a week, dinner became a 'Mess Night', when we dressed in our 'Blues' with the white starched jacket of tropical dress kit, and ate with some formality, and the junior subaltern proposed 'The Queen', and the port circulated clockwise, and it would have been unthinkable to produce cigarettes in a packet, not a case, and all that. On Mess Nights no one was allowed to leave before the colonel. Quite often he would suggest those notorious and incredible after-dinner games: not charades, but the brutal, military kind, involving drunken horseplay with cricket bat, polo stick, or tennis ball, and much wrestling and fighting, calculated to exhaust the randiest subaltern.

For the same reason the colonel also thought up the Escarpment Run. A book was kept at the door of the Mess in which were recorded the date and time of runs to the top of the Escarpment and back. It appeared quite close, but actually even the foot of the cliff was about a mile from the camp, across soft, uneven sand; and the track to the top was sheer and rough. I cannot remember how long the run took, but the best times, I believe, were something under an hour. It was very like the traditional Lake District sport of fell racing, and it seemed to me, for whom long-distance running is protracted torture, more of a punishment. Some of the older, overweight men came back in a dangerous state. The intention was to make the trip regularly, improving your time, aiming to be Escarpment Champion. One or two really keen types welcomed the exercise; others muttered but went on. Officially it was a voluntary run, but regular officers know they need the good word of their C.O. for promotion, and most of them set out keenly and frequently enough.

We National Servicemen though had nothing to lose. Most of us were only waiting to hear from GHQ that there was a seat for us on the plane back to England. I myself never made that run to the top of the Escarpment; as far as the colonel was concerned, it merely confirmed, I am sure, an unsuitability he had already guessed from other things: my service cap was unfortunately just not quite right; I was rather overweight; some of my civilian clothes were also not from the right places; my conversation revealed an ignorance of the expected topics—those clues by which a gentleman can tell you are not a gentleman.

However, even the Escarpment was not sufficient sublimation. Hysteria revealed itself in small things: petty jealousies, quick tempers, bickering over protocol and minor differences—the score at tennis, the order of service at the bar. The Mess was divided over whether the Sunday papers, which arrived from England in the middle of the week, should be put out at once or saved until the next Sunday. The debate grew out of all proportion, a passionate and intense division over a simple decision. There was some sort of feminine extravagance in this emotional intensity, and it reached a kind of climax one night when one of the officers, captain of a team in the Mess Night Games—this game, significantly, involved crawling under a bed, brought in from one of the tents—was so enraged at the slackness of one of his side that he slapped his face.

The young regular officers, fresh from Sandhurst, seemed all to have received their sexual initiation at the establishment of a certain Mrs F——, in South Kensington. Even the locality was respectable. This was the proverbial brothel of male myth, where all the girls were ladies, discreet, passionate, sympathetic; they asked you if you were *sure* you would not like them to stay a little longer, and then you slept until breakfast was brought to you in bed next morning. The only risk you ran was of being introduced to a girl you knew socially or—the pinnacle of this tradition— your sister. One man reported he had been told by his girl that he had 'nice firm testicles'—an expression that displayed much taste, if a somewhat desperate desire to please.

So when I got back to England I decided to visit Mrs F——. I found her name in the telephone book, discreetly listed as 'Mrs F——, Hotel'. I telephoned, from a call box, and said I'd been recommended by Mr X, and could she put me up for next Saturday night? 'Yes, of course,' she said. 'Should I be alone?' I understood *that* innuendo. 'Yes, I shall be alone.' My heart had been pounding when I started, but now I was calmly worldly. This was how it was done. 'Can you come about six,' she said, 'and I'll let you have a key?' This was exactly as I expected. At that six o'clock rendezvous there would be a girl. We should be introduced. I would casually mention the time I expected to come in that evening. And when I did, the girl would come to the room ...

I found the house in the wide terraces of South Kensington. Mrs F—— herself opened the door. (Where was the maid with the starched apron?) Mrs F—— was soberly elegant, warm in that relaxed and confident way that has just an edge of the perfunctory – the wife, you would guess, of a gentleman businessman. In the pocket of my coat I had a razor and toothbrush, sufficient for the morning. In my wallet was the necessary ten pounds and some to spare. Having progressed so far, I felt quite confident, and I followed Mrs F—— into the drawing-room with a pleasing exhilaration. There was a fire in the grate, and a comfortably chintzy air about the room – but no girl. Mrs F—— talked for a couple of minutes, but I scarcely listened. She told me where my room was, but did not offer to show it to me. 'What time do you think you're likely to be coming in?' 'Oh – about eleven,' I said. 'In that case I think I'd better give you a key ... ' The ritual was unfolding as if it had been rehearsed. 'And now,' she soon said, discreetly hurrying, 'I'm so sorry, if you'll excuse me, I have to go out shortly ...' I left. Obviously the girl had not turned up. Or was 'busy'. I supposed it did not particularly matter. Perhaps it was even better not to have met the girl before. I was damn sure it would not turn out to be *my* sister.

I only wondered how I could make the time pass between then and eleven o'clock. Somewhere in the West End I sat through a film, without seeing it. I got back to South Kensington, like Cinderella, as the hour struck. The house was silent and I blundered about noisily, looking for my room. It turned out to be bare — clean but shabby, with a strong and pervasive smell of rubber. Even the bathroom had the same slightly sour smell — the relic, I guessed, of thousands of rubber sheaths, used and discarded. Should I need one? I had not anticipated that. Well, they would have to provide it. Now I could hear sounds of activity — running water and creaking boards. I hurried to undress. I did not want to get caught like a bedroom farce, half out of my trousers, tangled in my braces. Waiting in bed, I smoked a cigarette. It seemed the right thing to do. The noises continued. Elsewhere, evidently, there was considerable activity. A busy night. That would explain the delay. But I was beginning to have doubts. Should I have told someone I was there? There was a telephone beside the bed. Should I call Room Service? And what should I say if I did? So I waited. Half an hour. An hour. All night. No one came.

And in the morning, as I left, I found Mrs F—— in the drawing-room, dressed for the street. She asked me if I had slept well. She took thirty shillings from me. In her presence it was out of the question to mention, even by polite allusion, such hideous realities as 'brothel' or 'prostitute'. She came to the door with me. Perhaps I should like to share her taxi? She was going to Harrods, if that was any help. No, I said, thank you, I was going the other way.

British sexual attitudes also demonstrate those habits that have given us a name for hypocrisy: that concern with appearances, that indirectness, that ambivalence — the difference between the description and the act. Men claim to respect women, but they both fear and despise them, ruthlessly denying them rights — not even equal pay for equal work. Pornography and prostitution are illegal, but even open transactions, if discreet, are tolerated. The taboo is verbal. Even 'knickers' is a naughty word, but the advertisements that line Underground escalators astound foreign visitors. Say one thing and do another: that's the English way. Logically that is dishonest, but rationalization makes honest liars of us all. It *is* a form of dishonesty, but it avoids confrontation with uncomfortable truth. The English are delicate about such confrontations.

In recent British history two Lawrences have been prominent—T. E. and D. H. I have always confused them. I once bought a copy of the letters of Lawrence of Arabia ('the last right-wing intellectual', Orwell called him), mistakenly expecting to read the correspondence of the novelist, D. H. I am not sure if they did meet, but certainly in that strange claustrophobic society in England around the time of the first war, they had friends and acquaintances in common. I think my confusion is apt. I'd like to think of them coming away from dinner with, say, Eddie Marsh, putting on their coats, and between hall and street merging into one person—and becoming the persona of English male sexuality, that rather edgy obsession with the devil in the flesh.

Both were noticeably small men, both remained boyish: T. E. with his smooth face (by some reports, he needed to shave only three or four times a year); D. H. impatient, selfish, petulant, with his enthusiasm and his tantrums. Both were mother-dominated. Both quick-tempered, with a streak of sarcastic and cruel humour. Both had that British, rather feminine attraction to intrigue—quick to suspect it, and take offence, and delighting to make plots themselves. Both were obsessed with dirt: D. H. himself, when he and Frieda arrived at new houses in Cornwall, Germany, Italy, Sicily, Australia, was on his knees, scrubbing out the dirt Frieda was too casual to see. And T. E., mortifying the flesh: 'I came here to eat dirt until its taste is normal to me!'

But the core of their essential Britishness lies in that uneasy sense of evasiveness, both in the lie direct (T. E. to the Arabs) and in that indefinable but definite sense of a man not telling the truth, and covering up for some sexual insecurity. Both had a horror of being touched: the English hysteria, *Noli me tangere*. Both were prudish in speech and behaviour. With T. E. the contradiction of that position has recently become evident. Already the published version of his treatment by the Bey of Deraa reads like homosexual masochistic fantasy: 'a Circassian riding whip ... thongs of black supple hide, rounded, tapering from the thickness of a thumb at the grip (which was wrapped in silver, with a knob inlaid with black designs) ... ' He 'confessed' another version to Bernard Shaw's wife, in which he explained, most delicately, that he had actually allowed himself to be buggered. And we have learnt since of later masochistic practice, *le vice anglais*, excused by the elaborate fiction of a disciplinary uncle. 'I'm fit now to take a few on the buttocks, if that's what the old man wants.'

And D. H. for all his declaration that 'the real way of living is to answer one's wants,' is unconvincing as the champion of sexual liberation. Preoccupied with those two English obsessions, sex and class, he is too strident, as if trying to convince himself—this little, driven man and his heavy, aristocratic wife. Advocating sexual freedom and earthy lovers, proposing the climax of sexual fulfilment in the buggery of Lady Chatterley, he nevertheless was inhibited and easily shocked, and swore to the permanence of marriage. His arguments for freedom sound like the description of what he would have liked for himself. That is legitimate and natural—but Lawrence would not admit it. He accused others of 'sex in the head', but he was guilty of it himself.

A frightening vision arises of this composite Lawrence, driven by a demon of sexual tension, intense and persuasive, rationalizing political activity, imperialism, social reform—for the sake of some private anal excitement, subconscious worship at the posterior shrine.

6. *A Dog I Know*

Nature and Nature's laws lay hid in night;
God said, *Let Newton be!* and all was light.
Alexander Pope (1688–1744)

No arrogant man was ever permitted to see Nature in all
her beauty.
John Constable (1776–1837)

Away with spleen and let us sing
The praises of the English Spring.
John Davidson (1857–1909), *St George's Day*

None of the other nations of Europe has so abject an
inferiority complex about its own aesthetic capabilities as
England.
Nikolaus Pevsner, 1955

On my father's three-acre island the environmental battle was engaged even then, twenty-five years ago. Kingfishers were nesting in the banks of the river. Spotted flycatchers chose the tennis post as a vantage point on summer evenings. I was once almost struck in the face by a sparrow-hawk, hedgehopping in the orchard. But, hopping back, the hawk would have been as likely to meet the windscreen of a parked lorry: on the other side of the thick privet hedges, three-tonner chassis, the garage vehicle stock, were already drawn up in the paddock. We kept various hens that were released to forage in the paddock, and the White Leghorns and Light Sussex were soon grey and oily from the yard. Occasionally we would find a broody hen on a nest of eggs in the cab of an old car, written off in a crash and abandoned.

I was somewhat preciously offended by this encroachment. Without any notion of the economic arguments, I could simply see the possibility of a beautiful garden, and refused to understand how a new engine shop, say, could be as important as the old mulberry tree. If I had had my way, the yard would have been screened from the paddock — there was not even a fence between them — and the garden extended, two acres along the bank of the river. What capabilities there!*

Mine was the sheer romantic view, a secret dream. I was too young to be involved in the business calculations, and

* Capability Brown, the great eighteenth-century landscape gardener, got his nickname from his habit of saying, when confronted with a new terrain, 'I see great *capability* of improvement here.'

every building that went up pained me, another blemish on my picture of the garden perfected. I developed a very unboyish aversion to machinery.

The whole town was similarly poised between city and country. In many ways it was like a village. On the marsh opposite our house, men would illegally net the goldfinches that flocked on the thistle-heads; little Mr Parsons, the shoemender, never had our shoes finished by the time he had promised, so his vast wife (they were a real comic-postcard couple) would walk them down to the house when they were ready; the hiring fair was still held at Easter in front of the church, and my father could remember when men actually came there to find farm work for the summer. And every Tuesday was market day, an exciting day, punctuated with the squeals of pigs—they squealed when their ears were pierced (and bled considerably), they squealed when the farmers twisted their tails and steered them out of their pens, they squealed when they were driven over the road to the slaughterhouse on the other side. There I never ventured, but my brother at one time was a regular visitor—to my mother's horror when she discovered it. If a pig or a couple of steers escaped into the town, as they sometimes did while being driven across to slaughter, people would mention it as an item of interest.

In those ways it was a country town. But it was besieged country. You had to travel several miles before you could find the fields and woods of actual countryside. Even if I had saved the paddock from the Leyland invasion, it would have been a pointless victory. That was not the place for countryside. At best it could only have been a pretence. London had already reached out and zoned those three acres for 'light industrial' use. Now the mulberry tree has gone, the house is demolished, even the river has been diverted.

It is not too fanciful, I think, to nationalize this ambivalence. Every nation has to be affected by its geography. We inhabit a small island, in an intermediate zone, moist* but comparatively mild, and without extremes of temperature. It is perhaps even true that four hundred years ago, when summer and winter were extremer seasons, we were bolder and more extreme in character. Annually roasting an ox on the Thames is part of the national mythology. It was Elizabeth I, of course, whose patronage in 1564 inaugurated the regular 'Frost Fairs'. It was not only a matter of climate: the old London Bridge stemmed the flow of the river, and it froze more easily.

At any rate, ours is now a hospitable landscape, without great mountains or impassable ranges, without deserts or impenetrable forests, without dangerous beasts or — with one rather shy exception — poison snakes. The land responds well to husbandry. But it does require attention. We all know, as Samuel Johnson said: 'When two Englishmen meet, their first talk is of the weather.' In a variable climate where, say, a good year for strawberries, or roses, depends on a lucky spell of weather at the right time, where a hard winter can kill most of the rosemary in the country, the weather becomes news as well as a safe topic of conversation. Snippets of country weather-lore are common knowledge: a heavy crop of berries means a hard winter; if it rains on St Swithin's day you can expect it wet for forty more;

> The oak before the ash
> There'll only be a splash.
> The ash before the oak
> You'll get a reg'lar soak

> If Candlemas day be fair and bright
> Winter will have another fight.
> But if Candlemas day brings cloud and rain,
> Winter is gone and won't come again.

There are scores of such rubrics.

* On a recent thirty-year average, England measured 32·7 inches of rain a year, Wales 53·4 and Scotland 48·8.

Lighting bonfires to keep the frost from the apple blossom, piling bracken on the crowns of tender plants, lifting our dahlia tubers, our begonias, wintering our geraniums under cover: naturally when our gardens require so much attention we have developed a strong affection for them, as one does for a child. There are times when you could believe from English conversation that the world will be saved when we get the roses blooming perfectly.

We are a town and country nation. ('Sir – May I, a townswoman,' writes a correspondent to the *Guardian*, 'write in favour of the threatened Yorkshire buttercups?') The Industrial Revolution created the distinction, and that industrialization is still recent enough, and the scale of our geography small enough, for us to be able to satisfy the yearning for rural contact. Emotionally we are not reconciled to the industrial monster we have created. We try to pretty it up with country touches. Stationmasters and lock-keepers pride themselves on their gardens; slum houses too grow cottage gardens, keep pigeon lofts and caged birds. * Even in cities, our buildings try to preserve the sense that each family occupies an entire house set in a leafy garden. Did we not invent that triumph of rural wishful thinking, the picnic?

In my family's marginal habitat, we did not know the 'real' country, in spite of our Sunday-afternoon expeditions to primrose woods, or the lane where, in spring, the banks were thick with white violets. Only when I went away to school, to those once-grand country houses, did I begin to appreciate true country matters. As happens to schoolboys, we went through crazes – stars, stamps, butterflies, cigarette cards, marbles – but it is the knowledge of natural history that has stayed with me. As I grew older, in the holidays, I began to work in the garden. When we pulled out 'the laurels' we began to grow gardener's plants. We didn't

---

* Some wit has said, with a certain truth, that the upper classes shoot birds, the middle classes protect them, and the lower classes cage them.

know the language, we were ignorant of the Latin nomen-
clature, but we learnt—after some ridicule: for years I
pronounced 'cotoneaster' as I read it from the catalogue,
until the mother of a school-friend put me right ('cotōn-e-
aster'). But it would not have been thought right to spend
money buying flowering plants. New asparagus roots were
a legitimate expense, but flowers had to be accumulated by
begging or the accepted English crime of stealing cuttings
from public gardens. Our plants were named from their
origin: we grew Mrs Haylock's azalea, Mrs Sweetenham's
iris and her carnation, the spirea from Woburn; they still
grow, under those names. By a few hundred yards we lived
in Essex. 'This whole county', wrote Count Friedrich
Kielmansegge in his diary after a visit in 1761, 'is not unlike
a well-kept garden.' Yet none of this quite explains the fact
that from somewhere I have inherited that English pleasure
in Nature, a delight in things that grow.

With Nature the British have always felt safe. Gardening
indeed is the English obsession. 'Without a garden,'
Francis Bacon said, 'building and palace are but gross
handiworks.' The art is perfect for the British taste, being
painstaking, and practical, requiring some physical effort,
and with the results easily measured. 'Sir,' writes Miss
Coode to *The Times* from Minchinhampton Stroud, 'I
have just measured one of the blooms on a rosebush in my
mother's garden here. It is Eden Rose, and is $7\frac{1}{4}$ in. in
diameter. One of Peace's blooms measures 7 in. Are these
records and is this a record year for glorious roses?' It
seems all was well in Gloucestershire in the summer of
'71.

It is in gardening that the English created their only
original art: the romantic landscape garden, that demon-
strates the principle, Horace Walpole said, that Nature
abhors a straight line. Nature makes the rules of beauty, and
the landscape gardener manipulates Nature to imitate herself. Of the garden at Dynevor, in Wales, Capability Brown

said approvingly, 'Nature has been truly bountiful, and art has done no harm.' Art, Pope agreed, 'is only like a prudent steward that lives in managing the riches of Nature.' 'Nature I loved, and next to Nature, Art.' British art is indeed next to Nature — so close that the two are sometimes confused. For that art requires those small deceptions that seem to be a part of British nature. In the gardens at Sissinghurst, famously beautiful, the nut wood is carpeted with polyanthus, as if growing there naturally; but actually Lady Nicolson had them under close control, weeding out undesirable forms that resulted from natural crossing, allowing only the best and certain restricted colours to flourish. That is the basis of British art: making tactful adjustments to Nature.

For the British, thinking themselves a practical nation, yet have a strong romantic streak. But they do their best to make it look down-to-earth. Art for art's sake: that condemnation betrays the fear of giving way altogether to the romantic urge. Art must rise out of practicality; it must never be considered to be basically important, never presume to claim to be the purpose of life, but merely a decoration. Art is not work: 'Another damned thick square book! Always scribble, scribble, scribble! Eh, Mr Gibbon?' scoffed the Duke of Gloucester. J. M. Barrie overheard two men talking about him once: 'He's not a playwright,' said one of them. 'I used to work with his father.'

The English visual arts are decorative, painstaking minor arts: tapestry, marquetry, portrait miniatures, wood-carving, illumination. Embroidery, on the Continent, was known as *opus Anglicanum* (with *Englischer garten* and *le vice anglais* making a trio that tells much about our reputation abroad). English taste is restrained taste. We do not go in for grand gestures. We never felt comfortable with that passionate Baroque painting. Our great nature painters, the portraits of Reynolds and Gainsborough, the animal portraits of Stubbs, are romantic *and* factual. Abstract art is uncompromising, an urban product and an American aberration. The British are suspicious of it, forever peering to work out some scenic interpretation. 'I make my surfaces smooth,' wrote Philip King, a modern British sculptor, in the catalogue for his show in Paris in 1968, 'because texture would get in the way, being loaded with information about the history of the material and revealing all sorts of facts about how long it took to make the work, what tools, etc.' But most Englishmen are discomfited by such art. They want the information. They only accept the abstract forms of Henry Moore and Barbara Hepworth if they can see the history in adzed wood, or laboriously worked stone—and preferably in some form that gives a hint of allusion to Nature.

'Take a word like "culture"—an abstract, difficult word. The English don't like it at all, and only use it with embarrassment,' apologized Richard Hoggart, then the British Assistant Director of UNESCO. When philosophy was a practical science, in the early days of the Royal Society, the British—men like Newton, Boyle, Bacon, Locke, Halley—excelled in it. Religion itself was susceptible to reason: indeed Locke wrote under the title *The Reasonableness of Christianity*. But abstract philosophy we have tended to leave to the Germans, whose language, we think, with its portmanteau words, is suitably turgid. Art and culture are the nursemaids of society: all very well in their place. 'Philosophy, by wandering far away into invisible notions, has almost quite destroyed itself.' That was the judgment of Robert Hook, in 1665, in a paper published by order of the Royal Society.

The Englishness that these things represent is the Englishness of the eighteenth century. The spirit of that age was powerful enough to aspire to become national character, replacing and refining much of the previous Tudor Englishness. It was recycled in the nineteenth century, but like recycled paper, it contains much the same elements, rearranged. The real change will have taken place when it is replaced by, to give it a name, American Englishness. But such substitutions take place gradually. We are still recognizably the heirs of the century that gave us 'landskip or picturesque gardening'; that most famous English poem, Gray's 'Elegy Written in a Country Church-yard'; the vogue for porcelain and *chinoiserie*, and the founding of Josiah Wedgwood's pottery; the English novel; the English school of painting – the portraits of Reynolds and Gainsborough, * the commentaries of Hogarth (who once signed himself 'Britophil'), Constable and the other East Anglian landscape painters; Methodism and the great Protestant revival; seaside holidays; English gin; the deifi-cation of the horse, and George Stubbs, iconographer of horseflesh; Dr Johnson, another John Bull, but with a prodigious brain; the perfection of domestic Palladian architecture, with its famous decorator, Robert Adam; the English breakfast; drinking tea and coffee; and the beer pull.

These days have given rise to another rich fantasy world of English society. Particularly from abroad, it looks un-commonly attractive.

> Sir Edward was so splendidly the Englishman of her dreams. The Englishman, freshly shaved, pink, shin-ing, groomed, and polished, facing the first rays of the morning sun in an already perfect white cravat, the Englishman of waterproof and mackintosh. Was he not the very crown of civilisation? ... I shall have English silverware, she thought, and Wedgwood china. There will be carpets all through the house and

---

* Gainsborough most often painted his subjects, elegantly dressed, in a rural setting. He painted the figures for money, and the backgrounds for his own satis-faction. 'I am sick of Portraits,' he wrote in a letter in 1770, 'and wish very much to take my viol-da-gamba and walk off to some sweet village where I can paint land-skips and enjoy the fag-end of life in quietness and ease. But these fine ladies and their tea-drinkings, dancings, husband-huntings etc etc etc will fob me out of the last ten years.'

powdered footmen, and I shall take the air at the side of
my husband driving in our four in hand through Hyde
Park ... Tame spotted deer will play on the green lawn
of my country house ...

This is the English dream of a nineteenth-century French
girl, heroine of a story by Théophile Gautier.

For me it is important that English landscape painting is
an East Anglian product. I cannot pretend that I was ever
aware of the particular quality of our light before it was
demonstrated to me, nor even of the modest beauty of the
landscape. It never presents itself to me as the pattern for
art, the vista that looks like a picture. But the paintings
celebrate not the artistic quality of the landscape, but the
beauty of its parts, its trees, clouds, grasses, weeds, even
individual leaves. That is where the real beauty lies: in the
texture of the plants. Constable, it was said, would stand
'gazing at the bottom of a ditch, and declare he could see
the finest subjects for painting.'

English landscape paintings, especially the watercolours,
project themselves modestly. But the simplicity is deceptive.
The intention of these understated paintings is never immediately clear. In his painting of Stoke-by-Nayland, for
instance—the quintessentially English picture—Constable
seems to show an arbitrary slice of typical country. But it
was very carefully worked out as a set-piece exhibition
painting, always a terrible challenge for Constable. The
landscape was rearranged and painted in at least two final
versions. The viewer is at first puzzled by this simple record
of trees and wayside grasses. It looks a very naïve picture.
But it is not. 'This is not drawing but inspiration!' ex-
claimed William Blake when he saw Constable's work. 'I
meant it for drawing,' said Constable deflatingly.

Samuel Johnson hated the countryside. Gilbert White of
Selborne dedicated his whole life to natural history. These
two are the town and country men of the eighteenth

century, and, at least in their manner, another pair of John Bull and Jack Beaver. As far as Samuel Johnson is concerned, his contradictory character makes it dangerous to claim him typical of anything. To his contemporaries he was certainly a hero, but we have chosen to remember him in the version that suits us: a mythical hero, more revealing of our character than his. We remember that he was rude, first of all, with a frequent play of robustly masculine sarcasm that we still quote with delight; that he preferred to argue always from practical examples, choosing fact before theory ('The value of any story depends on it being true.' 'I would rather see a portrait of a dog I know, than all the allegorical painting they can show me in the world'); he was obstinate, greedy, uncouth, untidy, unclean, but nevertheless quite endearing; he was disconcertingly honest, refusing even to let his servant lie that he was 'not at home'. We regard him with such affection because we have chosen to remember him as the proof that a man can eschew fancy manners, dislike pictures, hate the French, insult his friends and criticize Shakespeare ('Shakespeare never has six lines together without a fault'), yet still remain the hero of his age. There is a painting by Zoffany of Johnson at tea with the Garricks on the lawn of their villa at Twickenham, which embodies much of this eighteenth-century Englishness—tea on the lawn with the spaniels, the fisherman, the pastoral landscape, the weeping willows. Yet Dr Johnson is the centre of attention. And he is sitting in for all of us, proving that John Bull can hold his own, indeed is superior to elegant society, can quieten their gossip by his presence and his uncouth honesty. We have exploited him to excuse our own shortcomings.

Gilbert White, on the other hand, was a real old maid. But he was also stubbornly selfish and shrewd. He wrote vigorous and masculine prose on domestic, miniature subjects. His special study was concerned with the whereabouts of swallows in winter. He thought for a long time that they hibernated under water, and was never wholly convinced that some at least did not. He was kind to his relatives and the village folk, but wantonly cruel, in the manner of the time, to the birds and animals he had such affection for. If he wanted to study a bird, he had a few shot. His whole life was dedicated to the meticulous record of his observations of the natural life of the village. He was a charming, fastidious, private and quite selfish man. That also is the English manner.

It is no coincidence that Johnson would 'rather see a portrait of a dog I know'. We English have found the dog our ideal companion. It allows displays of affection – in both directions – of which we can control the occasion, alternately loving and whipping. It is also the type of animal that allows us to believe that the relationship is basically practical. Dogs have their uses, as guard-dogs, sheepdogs, in fox-hunting, bull baiting, retrieving, coursing; without his bull-dog at his side, John Bull is only half complete. We tend to despise decorative dogs – lap-dogs for old ladies – and pre-fer working varieties, however unlikely it is they will be called on to perform the function they were bred for. There must be thousands of Jack Russell terriers, bred for driving foxes and rabbits from their holes, living now in cities.

With the old sporting dogs we connect again with the vision of ourselves as robust Elizabethans. Though actually we are absurdly sentimental with animals. The world laughs at us and our pets, and we know it, but we don't mind. With a certain diffident satisfaction we admit to being silly over them. 'British Ponies Eaten on Continent', the papers headline. The Royal Society for the Protection of Animals, under royal patronage, gives a commendation for saving a goldfish from drowning. 'The novelist Olivia Manning', reports *The Times*, 'is selling her oil shares in protest of the widespread fouling of seabirds. "If our own cats and dogs were coming in like that, something would

be done." ' Ladies leave money for holiday homes for working horses, or to keep their dogs in luxury for life, or for
The Donkey Sanctuary —a registered charity with an ever-
open door. Relationships with a horse or a dog are easier
than human encounters, the judgment being entirely on the
terms of the owner. And those terms are adaptable without
public humiliation. Dog owners start with the intention
of keeping the creature in the yard, but they quickly give in
to pleading looks, and the dogs are in the house, in the
sitting-room, on the sofa, sleeping on the bed ... On cold
nights my father, somewhat shamefacedly, would warm the
dog's blanket at the fire and wrap him in it before he went
off to bed himself. We even used to take the dog for a 'walk'
in the car, driving out to fields or woods where he could
have a clear run. It had the advantage of giving this form
of leisure a satisfactory sense of duty.

With horses the relationship is necessarily less intimate,
since you can scarcely let a horse sleep on the bed —much
as many young girls would like. And that is part of the secret.
The attractions of the horse are anthropomorphic. Consider
the ideal horse —perhaps as Stubbs shows it in those great
pastoral paintings: the mares with their firm, round
haunches like women's buttocks; their large, liquid eyes;
the guarded expression of their faces; their soft mouths
(their breath, surely, warm and clean); hair falling round
their ears and over their foreheads; their warm smooth
bodies, with softly rounded bellies; their long elegant legs.
The physicality of horses is complementary in human terms.
You could equally describe a stallion to sound like Hercules.
No wonder eating horseflesh to the English seems akin to
cannibalism. Englishmen know about horses, or at any
rate believe they do. Many believe they are born with an
instinctive judgment of horseflesh (that is, as it means to
an Englishman, the quality of the living animal). King
Arthur owed his success to his cavalry, and we have
been famous as horse-lovers ever since. A tank may

be more useful in battle, but never a friend, as a horse can. For ceremony we prefer to keep the Household Cavalry.*

I was introduced to the horse, as to so many English traditions, on difficult terms, and we have always had a rather nervous relationship. A dog I could take or leave. In fact I only once had a dog – a Sealyham, given to me for my birthday when I was a child. I thought of it not as mine, but as the family's dog. One day it disappeared in the town and never came back. I was only briefly unhappy. Horses though, even if I never owned one, have always seemed to demand far more from me than I can give, and that challenge has kept the relationship alive.

I first met the horse – if one discounts donkey rides – at my Devon prep school at the age of seven. This was hunting country. The hunt met once a season in front of the school house, and doubtless there were horses all over the place. I don't know how, in that disorganized establishment, I actually found myself on the back of one, but I surely did. I vividly remember the horse they picked for me at the stables. It was a roman-nosed creature, solid and stubborn as a mule, with cast-iron ribs and matching temperament. It simply seemed impervious to the usual forms of encouragement. Its top gear was the trot. Now and then, abruptly, it would decide to stand still; then nothing would move it. They entered me on this beast for the bending race at a gymkhana, and at the last moment I was given a crop and told to use it if need be. But it made no difference. Halfway along the course the mulish creature stopped dead, and my beating and kicking seemed only to make it the more determined not to move. Eventually, when I had given up, it ambled to the finish. They gave me a green rosette for perseverance.

On that pony too I made my first appearance on the

* At the back of the coronation procession of Elizabeth II travelled a horse ambulance, in case of a fall on the wet roads.

hunting field.* I believe we children only followed for part of the day; I am sure I was never blooded — I doubt anyway if anyone could have got that pony as far as the death. It had started with a frightening excitement, tearing away with me as if to show that its usual laziness was a calculated insult, though doubtless sooner or later it would have taken it into its head to stop in its tracks for half an hour here and there ... the memory is vague, for some very good reason, I am sure.

In any event, I seem surprisingly to have acquired a taste for the sport. It was not long before it became a weekly event for my mother to take us, my brother and me, and later me and my sister, in jodhpurs and hacking jacket, five or six miles to Mr Rimes's stables. There was a field attached to the school, and we sometimes rode there, learning to jump as we became more secure in the saddle. There was no open country for us to ride out in. If we wanted a long gallop we had to go along the side roads until we came to the arterial road to Cambridge and there gallop along the wide grass verge. This stable was midway between home and the school I went to when I was thirteen, and it took boys from there too. Mrs Rimes came once a week and collected boys from the porter's lodge and took them for the lesson. For a year or so I attended, walking across the quad to the lodge in my riding kit with some self-consciousness. But after a while I gave up. It was, as I said, a nervous pleasure. There was never any doubt between me and the horse as to who was the master on these occasions: it was the horse. And it was a pointless pastime. Again I was aware — vaguely then, clearly now — of doing a thing in the wrong way. It did not lead to my hunting, or racing, or show-jumping, or even being able to ride by myself across country. Those weekly hours were an end in

---

* You might care to know that hunting cries derive directly from Norman French: 'yoicks' from *'illoeques'* = *illo loco* = 'in that place'. 'Tally ho!' from *'ty a hillaut'* = *'il hist hault'* = 'He's up and away.'

themselves, another social asset carefully and expensively acquired. It merely enabled me to go for organized rides with girls of similar families that we met on holiday in Devon.

Oddly enough, riding did not seem to be a necessary qualification for the Royal Horse Artillery. No one asked if I knew the nose from the tail until I actually joined the regiment in Germany. There, two of us, both new arrivals, were summoned to the commanding officer. The other man (or boy—we were eighteen) was the son of a professional soldier, a friend of the C.O., so they were known to one another, fellow-members of the same club, and they exchanged a few words. Then the C.O. turned to me. He looked at my cap, frowned. 'You'll have to do something about that badge,' he said. 'Sir,' I mumbled, not knowing quite what could be wrong with it. Then he said, 'Do you ride?' 'Yes, sir,' I said. 'Good,' he said. Those two remarks were all the C.O. ever addressed to me. And although my answers were strictly truthful, I was aware that we were actually at cross-purposes. Riding, to that man, was not a thing you learnt at a suburban riding school, an hour a week; you learnt it at home, as a matter of course, since there were always horses around.

However, I was never called to demonstrate my skill. Although the regiment kept its own stable of horses, some of them available, if you had not brought out your own, for no more than three pounds a month—you telephoned the stables and a groom saddled your horse and brought it to the door of the mess—it soon turned out that virtually the only reason us National Service subalterns were accepted in this snobbish regiment was so that we could be responsible for morning maintenance parades. These unfortunately coincided with hound exercise—the regiment also had its own pack—for which senior officers liked to turn out on crisp mornings. Those regular officers regarded us enlisted men with open contempt. We had nothing in common, and much at extreme variance. 'When in close contact with officers of the Regular Army,' Siegfried Sassoon had written in 1928, 'I always found it a distinct asset to be able to converse convincingly about hunting. It gave one an almost unfair advantage in some ways.'

We English love Nature, but we love it more domesticated. There are fresh flowers in the house. Flower arrangement is the favourite art of middle-aged ladies, and arrangement is planned to look *casually* pleasing—a natural arrangement, unlike the formalized Japanese style. There are grassy parks in the cities, *rus in urbe*. The garden of Buckingham Palace is laid out like a country estate, with lawns and wandering paths and ornamental water—unlike the urban, geometric gardens of Continental palaces. On his return visit back to the country, the city dweller, secure in his miniature house on wheels, drives in company through a 'safari park', making safe contact with exotic wild life.

Rabbits, chickens (I had a pet hen called Blackie that was allowed in the garden), tortoises, ducks, geese, pigeons, pigs, ferrets, cats and dogs: at one time or another we had all of these. In the war I understood from my mother that, whenever we had rabbit pie, she had exchanged one of our live pets for a dead rabbit from the butcher. My brother showed me how to tell the sex of a rabbit. It involves some manipulation under the fur. One day I experimented with a young litter, taking them out of of the hutch one by one and holding them down while I felt excitedly for their organs—to discover that my brother had been watching me from behind a tree. 'Caught you!' he said triumphantly.

Nature in these tamed forms I experienced. Culture though, if that word has a useful meaning, I did not, even in the forms in which it might be thought to refer to Nature. Books were read occasionally, and in a passive manner. You never sought out a book. You read, or not, the books that came into your hands by chance. Similarly with the theatre: there were certain occasions for which a theatre visit was appropriate, and only when they arose would you begin to think what you might want to see. When my mother's father died, my mother inherited three very large paintings in elaborate gilded frames. They had hung, disproportionately large, in my grandfather's bungalow, adding, I guess, to the impression I had that he and Miss Wing lived in a slightly oversize house. We didn't know what these paintings were, though one clearly showed Abraham on the point of sacrificing his son. At any rate, two of them looked impressive in the recesses either side of the chimney in the drawing-room—another of those accidentally grand touches. The third, a portrait of a very matronly girl, hung at the top of the house. My sister and I, who passed it on the way to our rooms, referred to her as Fanny. Some years later I was surprised to find myself standing in front of her in the Uffizi in Florence: Titian's *Flora*. No pictures were ever bought, or for that matter even looked at, and that not because they were financially out of the question. China and glass and silver were bought, at some expense. But they can be used, if only on special occasions. A picture is a shameless luxury.

It follows that certain types of book are taken more seriously than others. Fiction is frivolous, except those classics that time has made respectable and so, useful, giving one 'education'. Instructive and improving literature is above suspicion. Penguin Books, along with the B.B.C. and possibly *The Times*, have become so important in British culture because of their evident intention to improve as well as, even instead of, entertain. No wonder that bird on Penguin Books wears a slightly uncertain expression.

If the landskip is our national visual art, poetry is its verbal equivalent. Again we seem to excel on the periphery, achieving greatness on the fringes of the real operation of life. Poetry is allusive and indirect. It is, we believe, prose with the adjectives interfered with, and its concern is verbal not political. In fact we treat poetry as we treat painting.

Damning it with faint attention, we agree that it can be 'nice', but we would never look to it for advice.

We tolerate poetry as a safety valve. The poetry in which the English have always excelled is romantic stuff, dealing with love, of women or Nature. We are reluctant to leave the maternal breast. And there, poetry allows itself unashamed romanticism, sighing and swooning to the song of nightingales. Constable's *The Hay Wain* is the English painting most often bought in reproduction, Gray's *Elegy* the most quoted poem. If there's one couplet we all remember from the schoolroom, it's 'The curfew tolls the knell of parting day/The lowing herd winds slowly o'er the lea.' (Onomatopoeia, neat Miss Lee informed us.)* Our most celebrated poets, Keats, Wordsworth, Shelley, Chaucer, Gray, Milton,† themselves celebrate the peculiarities of the English scene. They tread a dangerously narrow path between the moving and the soppy, unfairly susceptible to fashion and the reader's mood.

Rupert Brooke, at the Café des Westens in Berlin in 1912, had romantic memories of maytime Cambridge:

> —Ah God! to see the branches stir
> Across the moon at Granchester!
> To smell the thrilling-sweet and rotten
> Unforgettable, unforgotten,
> River smell, and hear the breeze
> Sobbing in the little trees.
> Say, do the elm-clumps greatly stand
> Still guardians of that holy land?
> Is dawn a secret shy and cold
> Anadyomene, silver-gold?
> And sunset still a golden sea

* The same poet's famous lines, 'Where ignorance is bliss,/'Tis folly to be wise,' are, happily, the last lines of the 'Ode on a Distant Prospect of Eton College'.
† Milton addressed *his* nightingale thus:
> 'Oh Nightingale, that on yon blooming spray
> Warbl'st at eve when all the woods are still ...'

From Haslingfield to Madingley?
And after, ere the night is born,
Do hares come out about the corn?
Oh, is the water sweet and cool
Gentle and brown above the pool?
And laughs the immortal river still
Under the mill, under the mill?
Say, is there Beauty yet to find?
And Certainty? And Quiet kind?
Deep meadows yet for to forget
The lies, and truths, and pain ... oh! yet
Stands the church-clock at ten to three?
And is there honey still for tea?

For all the accuracy of its adjectives, that's a public-school poem. George Orwell, predictably, did not like it: 'a sort of accumulated vomit from a stomach stuffed with place names.' As with so many of our patriotic poets, you wonder which Rupert Brooke really did love, his country or his countryside. The poem was written fifty years ago, and in that time it has become impossible to write again in that style. Yet, two hundred years before, in 1726, John Dyer had ended a similar poem:

And often, by the murm'ring rill
Hears the thrush, while all is still,
Within the groves of Grongar Hill.

The man who interviewed me when I went for a scholarship to Cambridge asked me if I liked Milton. 'Not really,' I said, sensing that I should somehow not be expected to. I'm sure I had never read any more that the parts of *Paradise Lost* reprinted in *The Oxford Book of English Verse*. He sighed and protested faintly that he found the poet sadly underestimated these days, a very great poet indeed. He himself, apparently a very shy man, lectured in a monotonous voice on the odes of Pindar. Milton perhaps was steamy stuff beside these ancient contorted compliments, written in praise of Olympic victors: 'Endued with that youthful beauty, which formerly with the aid of Venus averted the cruel fate of Ganymede ...' But much of the trouble is the failure of my own response. I am emotionally tone-deaf to poetry.

Naturally this causes some difficulty also in the matter of our national poet. It seems almost too easy to allow that he was a giant, and giants make exceptions to every rule. There are times when I resent the fact that Shakespeare hogs the limelight and dispossesses many good playwrights. I wish he had not been cried up to the point where audiences, knowing they are expected to admire, watch his plays in a nerveless trance. There are times when I think that to compose mock Shakespearean verse, with that relentless rhythm, those slightly off-centre prepositions, that alliteration and internal near-rhyming—it must be child's play.

Why do you bend such solemn brows on me?

His or mine? His plays are difficult to perform (some of them, to a modern audience, downright silly); he can be guilty of platitudes, of word-spinning. Yet, such beauty of language, such human wisdom ...

Apt that our national poet is a playwright, for we are good actors too. Once we persuade ourselves it is an acceptable pastime, and overcome our shyness, we are masters at this contrived escape from reality. The more artificial, the more eagerly we throw ourselves into it: we excel at verse drama, at farce, at the comedy of manners. In these forms it is obvious that the actor is not serious, he is performing, he can retain a sense of detachment, and we find this comforting, both sides of the footlights.

It is this holding back that restricts us in other arts. You can make a grand gesture only when you mean it passionately. Writing a good detective story, you are playing a game well. 'My interest in the macabre and suspenseful is a purely English thing,' says Alfred Hitchcock. 'Nobody in the

world is so obsessed with murder as the English.' But the
obsession is escapist: it is based on the assumption that murder is the very last thing we could actually get caught up in.

'Our general taste in England is for epigrams, turns of
wit and forced conceits,' wrote Joseph Addison in his *Specta-
tor*. 'Which have no manner of influence either for the
bettering or enlarging the mind of him who reads them.'
It is true the pun is our favourite sport. The conceits of
Oscar Wilde, the fey fantastic humour of Edward Lear and
Lewis Carroll, the absurdity of Gilbert and Sullivan, even
the adjectival torrent of Dylan Thomas, are all related: it is
a verbal, punning art. Who but an English soldier, after
the capture of Hyderabad in Scind in 1843, could send the
one-word cable: *Peccavi*. Sir Charles Napier knew that
everyone in the India Office had learnt Latin at school, and
would translate it, 'I have sinned.'

Often the pun becomes class-conscious, and then it is
even more specifically English. Mrs Malaprop's *faux pas*
are class jokes as well as puns. All families have malapro-
pisms that raise a smile whenever they are remembered.*
'Who is that lady I saw you with last night?' is a class-
conscious pun. As the bus stops in Piccadilly, the Cockney
conductor calls out, 'Green Park. The Ritz. Dinner is
served.' Cockney humour—and also a class pun. Cockney
rhyming slang is puns. Spoonerisms are straight puns.

The subject of our humour, when it is not straight ver-
balism, is a slightly cynical but essentially kindly view of
human foibles. We are known to be able to laugh at ourselves. That takes a deal of self-confidence and some double-
think. You only laugh at yourself if you are actually proud
of the way in which you are amusing. The perfect English
story concerns the Englishman who allows others to think
him a fool, but turns out in the end to be the wiser. We
know that in the end the jester has more wisdom than the

---

* Mine have included 'Dr Green's insulting room', 'very close veins', 'wire-front
pants'.

prophet. At times we exaggerate our eccentricity for that very purpose. Those ultra-R.A.F. types with handlebar moustaches that you still find in pubs are surely playing that game. Again, it keeps open the escape route: you can always pretend you were joking. We are afraid to take things too seriously.

We delight in foibles and privately we encourage eccentricity. It is a useful safety valve in a repressed society. We have supported it with our love of gossip. It is our private joke, for the family/nation and not for outsiders. Eccentricity is almost an aristocratic tradition. The middle class is the great destroyer of eccentrics. But in a sense also it creates them, since only a society requiring conformity judges anyone eccentric. There are certain accepted rules for the game. The basic rule is moderation: it is fine to hunt on the back of a bull with a pack of pigs, provided you do no harm and do not appear to want to convert others to the habit. Everyone loved John Lennon when he was just a little weird, but when he started preaching he very soon got to be a pain in the neck.

English art, seeing itself in contrast to an unaesthetic reality (Nature idealized through human nature), is anti-corporeal. Passionate William Blake, a genius disguised as an English amateur, celebrated physicality in words, but his drawings were of spiritualized bodies. Our artists have never excelled at sculpture—not, at least, while it was inevitably physical. Our diet produces flabby bodies, and our climate does not encourage us to bare them. We have been obsessed with nudity, have practised sex in the dark, and grown lazy about keeping control of beer bellies and bread hips. Traditionally we have taken more care for the covering than for the flesh: 'Must hasten to dress in my new plum-coloured suit,' wrote John Knyveton. 'I may even, in honour of the occasion, take a bath, though it be at this treacherous season of the year and I took one as recently as June'—only three months earlier. But that was two hundred years ago. A hundred years ago, according to *The Times*, 'Most persons in decent society content themselves with washing their face and hands in cold water twice a day, and their feet once a week.' Now almost 90 per cent of households have plumbed baths, and TV advertisements (over 90 per cent have TV sets) must have persuaded us to bath two or three times a week.

The size of our island imposes a certain homogeneousness on us. Isolated by the sea, we live in a secretive landscape of woods and enclosed fields. All of us can appreciate Constable's hedgerow, since similar hedgerows are found in Scotland as well as Suffolk. Our climate affects us. Directly it accounts, with its moist atmosphere, for the famous complexion of our women. Indirectly, for instance, our sheep, supported so generously by English grass, have given us a taste for lamb, and an attitude to wool that verges on reverence.*

When I was a child, if we had strawberries for tea, I had to eat them with bread and butter. They were considered too rich to eat alone. Perhaps unadulterated pleasure was thought dangerous. My father liked plain food, and he liked it hot. He was forever mumbling about the heat of the plates. He would even take the milk from the fridge the night before to make sure it did not make his tea cold in the morning. And if he had to make tea without giving the milk time to reach room temperature he would stand the bottle in hot water for a minute or two. Foreign food he was not

---

* Advertisements for wool, the merchants rightly realize, have no need to claim actual virtues. 'Pure new wool', they say, knowing none of us will dare say, 'So what?' We inherit generations of reverence for the commodity that first made England rich, that put us on the international map and started the processes that led us to the powerful days of industry and empire. In the stained glass in a wool merchant's house in Nottinghamshire is written:

> I thank God and ever shall
> It is the sheepe hath payed for all.

Those stupid animals have dominated our history, and dominated our politics, at home and abroad, for four hundred years. Yet 'sheep ate men': the sixteenth-century enclosures were made by farmers eager to increase their output of wool, and they took land that had supported men directly.

keen on: they did not even pretend to warm the plates. Risotto, say, would bring from him, 'What's this then?'

But none of us knew Continental food in those days, and no doubt he would have changed as we all have. As a child I scarcely knew what an omelette was. Eggs were boiled, fried, scrambled or poached (with haddock), but an omelette was a foreign device. Occasionally, when we stayed there overnight, Mrs Haylock would give us for breakfast a sort of Spanish omelette, with pieces of ham or bacon in it, and for many years that was what 'omelette' meant to me.

English food is home food. It is extravagant. We spend on average more than a quarter of our income on food. 'These Englishmen', a Spanish visitor mentioned in 1577, 'have their houses made of sticks and dirt, but they fare commonly so well as the king.' Success with English food depends on the best ingredients, freshly cooked. Its terrible reputation is founded on restaurant preparation. It cannot survive economy and early cooking. Roast beef 'kept warm' turns grey and tough. Yorkshire pudding should be cooked under the roast, turning out crisp and rusty with the juice of the meat. Potatoes are best inelegantly large, freshly cooked and floury—but they do not stay long in that condition. Pastry should be eaten from the oven. Fish and chips, tea, green vegetables—they all spoil by standing. And all, if cooked at perfection, need no sauces.

For years we have refused to face the fact that modern conditions do not support this cuisine. Now we are at last learning that Spaghetti Bolognese is tastier than mince and boiled potatoes—though we still eat more potatoes, by weight (two hundred and twenty pounds a year each), than any other food. Indeed, certain pretentious sections of society have taken to the Continental way with tactless zeal. Who has not been offered a simple English dish, like treacle tart, so disguised with lemon juice, nutmeg, wholemeal flour, cream and such as to be unrecognizable? That is what my father was suspicious of.

7. *The Rapid Car*

Soon shall they arm, UNCONQUERED STEAM! afar
Drag the slow barge, or drive the rapid car;
Or on wide-waving wings expanded bear
The flying chariot through the fields of air.
                              Erasmus Darwin (1731–1802)

The manufacturing system has already so far extended its
influence over the British Empire as to effect an essential
change in the general character of the mass of the people.
                              Robert Owen, 1815

We who lived before railways and survive out of the ancient
world are like Father Noah and his family out of the Ark.
                    William Makepeace Thackeray (1811–63)

I never spend five minutes enquiring if we are unpopular.
The answer is written in red ink on the map of the globe.
                              Lord Curzon (1859–1925)

It seems to me that the British character, after the eighteenth-century Englishman, got itself recycled again in quite quick succession by the Industrial Revolution and the British Empire. Cultural attitudes remained very similar, if not actually unchanged — Nature was still, and remains, the mirror to art. But industrialization, and all that red ink on the globe, emphasized other aspects of our character. This — broadly call it Victorian — cycle is that which is now drawing to a close. Indeed, lack of a convincing successor can be the only thing that keeps its influence alive.

One of the bridges between the two previous cycles is that romantic seam in our character, of which the surface is evident in the Nature of art: Nature dickered with, subtly anthropomorphized to satisfy human aesthetics. The paintings of Turner actually attempt to demonstrate a direct progress, from the 'improved' romantic landscape in imitation of the style of Claude Lorraine, to the romanticized industrial scene of *Rain, Steam & Speed — The Great Western Railway*. William Blake's 'Jerusalem' has become almost an alternative national anthem, sung at Women's Institute meetings, without fail, as the introductory hymn. Its full title is 'Jerusalem: the Emanation of the Giant Albion', and its famous vision of 'dark Satanic mills' was inspired by the Albion Steam Mills in London.

The dark and slimy underside of this metaphorical bridge was the Satanic side of the British character, the Gothic Romanticism of Byron, William Beckford, Shelley, 'Monk' Lewis, Swinburne and those people, flirting with death and the black games of incest, pansexualism, drugs ...

Her perfume thrilled and stung him; he bent down and kissed her feet ... which he took and pressed down on his neck. 'Oh! I should like you to tread me to death, darling ... I wish you would kill me some day: it would be so jolly to feel you killing me. Not like it? Shouldn't I? You just hurt me and see.' She pinched him so sharply that he laughed and panted with pleasure. 'I should like being swished even I think.'

You might guess this was a piece of pornography, but it is Swinburne; the novel, *Lesbia Brandon*; and the partners in the above exchange, brother and sister.

This dark Romanticism, this obverse of Nature — *un*natural vice — must also have seemed in tune with the growing convention of the two worlds of the nineteenth century, those two sides of the coin, 'polite society' and the 'facts of life'. Division was universal. While the Industrial Revolution developed, Romanticism flourished.

> And Joy, whose hand is ever at his lips
> Bidding adieu.

Keats caught that English misty melancholy nicely — himself mentally if not physically robust, yet 'half in love with easeful death'. And while he wrote this pale adolescent stuff they were already building the railways that in the next thirty years would cover six thousand miles of Britain. Mary Shelley conjured up Frankenstein: Manchester multiplied its population ten times in sixty years, building the hundreds of factories that poured black smoke into the air and cotton cloth at production level. Manchester was the nursery of that Victorian money arrogance: 'What Manchester thinks today, England thinks tomorrow.' Yet Engels, when he visited it, was convinced it would be the seed-bed of revolution.

On the day of my father's funeral the works were closed for the afternoon, and many of the men came up the road to the service in the Abbey. The same happened, even in 1970, when my brother died. Both times I see it in retrospect as a very Victorian scene, but at the time it seemed perfectly natural. It will not happen when the next managing director dies. My father was not managing director: he was the 'guv'nor'. Benevolent, certainly, but no less a tyrant. When I took to the law and was lectured on the concept of the separate entity of a company, I learnt of the vast body of company law that grew up to deal with the enterprises of the Industrial Revolution and the investment of the new industrial fortunes. I never mastered it, but I think I understood the concept easily enough. I am sure I do now. As things are the company seems a necessary legal creation. But I could never have explained it to my father—or indeed to my brother. My father would have given me that mystified, almost pitying look, which indicated that there was a lot about life that education could never teach you.

There were shares in the company, but what obligation could there be to pay dividends, when all were owned by him, or the family by his gift?—And who would say he did not provide adequately for his dependents? Trade unions, service contracts, profit sharing: they were not for his company. You employed accountants, not to give financial advice but to tidy up the finicky ends and produce a balance sheet, since the law and the tax-man required it. Why should he himself need a balance sheet? He knew every corner of the business, he read every timesheet, every job-card. Success or failure was easily measured: the Midland Bank was across the road and, though reluctantly trusted, their statement was sufficient guide. This simplistic attitude, this 'pound-note' mentality naturally caused troubles. When you stand back from it you can see, it is the major crisis such a company has to face, the transition from guv'nor to managing director. It must depend on the qualities of the guv'nor, and probably his family, but it seems that a garage can employ a hundred or so men, and at that size one man can keep control. Above that the company becomes another creature altogether, and that's the creature the Companies Act delineated.

'It's not the demand for motor-cars', says E. J. Hobsbawm, historian of the Industrial Revolution, 'existing in the 1890s which created an industry of the modern size, but the capacity to produce cheap cars which produced the modern man's demand for them.' This is a restricted truth, but within its limits, my father, and we his family, were the benefactors of those industrial processes. In fact the car itself, however sophisticated the system of its manufacture, remains a simple object. And that made the careers of my father, and the men he stands here for, possible.

The British heirs of the Industrial Revolution, until recently, have not had to be efficient. They were the first, and that, while they remained so, was enough. They were reluctant to move into new areas. Early technology was simple, and the village smith himself was expert enough to work on the machines it produced; when they went wrong it was smithy skill that put them right.* We have never learnt to trust machines. We need to be able to check on them by knowing how they work.

For the old machines, specialization was not needed. My father himself would stand patiently at the lathe, late into the night, turning a valve that would get a customer's car back on the road. (On the day of the General Strike, when he was due to drive a bus—already in 1926 he had aligned himself with the proprietors—a splinter of steel flew into his eye.) That attitude reveals itself still in the scant respect we have for design. Why pay some fancy fellow, we think, to indulge, at your expense, tastes he cannot afford himself?

---

* The motor trade is a secondary, parasitic trade, but I think it is nevertheless significant that smithy work—reconditioning engines, grinding valves, reboring cylinders—no longer takes place in the garage. The complete engine goes back to the manufacturer and is replaced by another, already treated.

In the late eighteenth century, the Peel family (they also came out of inn-keeping: the family had kept the Black Bull) founded a calico printing business. It was almost as directly profitable as printing money itself. Sir Robert Peel, a son, died in 1830, leaving a vast fortune of one and a half million pounds, and his own son to become Prime Minister. But for many years after the firm started to print, it had no design shop, and only the most primitive provision for deciding on the patterns. Similarly, my father rebuilt several of his workshops, and soon after his death my brother embarked on a considerable building programme. They neither of them employed an architect. Much of the time they preferred direct labour even to a building contractor. At least one building deteriorated quickly into a dangerous condition.

If he had known — perhaps he did — my father would have been satisfied that the pioneers of the Industrial Revolution were not all highly educated men. They were practical engineers. Brunel, James Watt, Thomas Telford, are well-known names, but George Stephenson is the folk hero of the railway age. He was pretty well illiterate, a John Bull figure, intolerant, vulgar and arrogantly confident. But he was a natural mechanical genius. He taught himself to read at the age of seventeen, and he learnt the principles of engineering by dismantling and putting together the steam-pumps that were then in use in the coal mines. He ended life as a world-famous figure, father of the railway.

His steam train, the 'Rocket', was entered for the Rainhill trials in 1829, a public contest set up by the directors of the projected Liverpool to Manchester line. They were doubtful whether locomotives could replace fixed steam-engines, and they needed visible proof. This was, after all, a most important stretch of line, the link between the great industrial centres of the revolution.

Twenty thousand people attended the trial run on two straight miles of track. A special stand was built to shelter the ladies. With George at the controls, the Stephenson Rocket, with yellow body and tall chimney with a petalled top, ran sweetly over the course, there and back, at an average speed of fourteen miles per hour. The Stephensons won the five-hundred-pound prize, and an order for six engines. The whole affair has an agreeable atmosphere, logical yet operatic. It seems a shame that we are too sophisticated for such antics now.

Like opera, these historic moments run the danger of turning out unintentionally comic. There were some odd entries in the original trials of the locomotives, and some explosive breakdowns. But the official opening of the railway itself on September 15th, 1830, was grotesquely comic. The Duke of Wellington, then Prime Minister, was to perform the ceremony: starting from Liverpool, seen off by enormous crowds and several brass-bands, he rode in a splendid carriage with a red interior and gilded laurel wreaths on the roof. Five trains took part, on the double track. They travelled at fifteen miles per hour ('as if on the wings of the wind', reported the *Liverpool Courier*) and they had no brakes. With the Duke in the ceremonial carriage was William Huskisson, M.P. for Liverpool. They stopped to watch one of the trains on the other track as it flew by. Huskisson foolishly got out on to the second line. The Rocket bore down on him, unable to stop, and crushed his leg. 'This is the death of me!' he cried. 'I am dying. Call Mrs Huskisson.' As the *Courier* correspondent put it, 'The feelings of this unfortunate lady can be imagined: they cannot be described.' Huskisson was rushed to hospital on one of the engines, with George Stephenson driving — at a speed of more than thirty miles per hour. Huskisson, however, died that night, and was subsequently buried in an iron grave. A hundred and fifty years later British Rail ran their last-ever steam-train over this same line. Great crowds turned out to see it pass. We have always had this affection for steam-engines, as if they were carthorses.

When industry turned to more sophisticated machinery, we withheld our enthusiasm.

The car was the afterthought of the Industrial Revolution. By the time of its arrival, Britain was already paying the price of being first. The inevitable leap-frogging of technology was taking place. While our investment was in that crude, thudding machinery, others ran up in our footsteps, sprang from our backs and landed ahead of us. But that did not matter too much to my father, developing a service, not a manufacturing industry. For him the timing was perfect. I guess business must have been slow at the start, when cars were privileged possessions.* At first he himself used only a motor-bike, with a sidecar for my mother. Then he and his brother bought the car they shared. But he was running in for the great motor-boom between the wars; when it came he was ready for it.

My father was lucky too, if you can call it that, in being unfit for military service in the first war. Petrol may have been rationed, and road use restricted, but at least he was there to keep an eye on things and to do the commercial work that was sanctioned for the war effort. I know nothing of the business then, but I know that the years of the second war and immediately after did show signs of prosperity for our family. Three children were at private schools. And those were the times when the silver tray came to the sideboard, the cut glass multiplied in the cupboard, and the reproduction Chippendale was replaced by better reproduction Hepplewhite round the dining-room table.

After the Industrial Revolution, the old world was certainly doomed. It was doomed by the plain working of history, as soon as land ceased to be the greatest wealth.

---

* Statistics: In 1910 there were fifty thousand cars in use in Britain, half a million in 1925, a million in 1930. Now there are more than twelve million. Quite sane forecasts expect that figure to double in the next ten years. Britain has a car for every five or so people, where in the U.S.A. there would be two. Yet Britain has more vehicles per mile on its roads than any other country: 62·6 per mile, compared to 28·6 in the U.S.A.

Both world wars gave the process a push. After the first war, some people even talked seriously about 'revolution'. In 1922, Lloyd George, then Prime Minister, said in the House of Commons that 'the country is facing a situation analagous to civil war.' But actually it was the usual British inability to understand one another across the class barrier. The workers wanted a decent wage and some sort of life; they had gone through the hell of Passchendaele and 'Wipers' and they felt entitled at least to that. Twenty-five thousand unemployed paraded on Armistice Day 1922 with a wreath on which they wrote: 'From the living victims – the unemployed – to our dead comrades, who died in vain.' In the General Strike of 1926 the trade unions were at pains to point out that they did not challenge the constitution, being engaged 'solely in an industrial dispute'. But the Government, and the ruling classes, thought they could feel a nasty draught and jumped to the conclusion that it blew from Moscow and the Bolshevik revolution. Had not the Bolsheviks proclaimed the 'dictatorship of the proletariat'? They were scared, and they took amazing steps to protect themselves. In 1919 troops and tanks were sent to Glasgow to face striking Clydeside workers. Later in the same year troops and tanks were sent to Liverpool, and H.M.S. *Valiant* and two destroyers were ready at hand in the harbour! The Home Secretary set up a force of 'Citizen Guards', in face of 'the menace by which we are confronted'. The next year, confronted by a strike of miners, railway men and general workers – the Triple Alliance – the Government assumed emergency powers as if for war. In 1921 the Army Reserve was called up and Defence Units were enrolled – to confront another strike, despite the assurance of the Triple Alliance that 'We are not proclaiming a revolution, we are standing shoulder to shoulder for fundamental trade-union rights.'

Hysteria in the ruling class took some ludicrous forms. A few days before this latest strike was due to take place, the

Recorder of London said to a man found guilty before him: 'The present condition of things is very alarming, and we may require the services of such men as you to defend the country against a foe perhaps quite as serious as the Germans whom we spent four years in fighting: therefore I cannot but be reluctant to send you to prison, where you would be of no kind of use to His Majesty.'

The ordinary working man had realized that he had misread the contract of war. He had understood it to mean a better life and a new society, in exchange for his blood. Now every time he asked for specific performance they called out the troops. And when he went to law, it turned out that the other party to the contract was also the court of appeal. No wonder the intellectuals of the 'thirties were attracted to communism.* I never understood until I read about these times the sullen and inflexibly extreme positions that each side took up and which still colour social attitudes. But those nine days of the General Strike are written on the hearts of my parents' generation. Unemployment was the bogey that kept them awake at night: in 1933 it touched three million.

The second war accelerated the natural process. Wartime camaraderie today sounds almost too good to be true. We all look back on those times with surprisingly rose-tinted glasses—even many of those who were on active service. You quite commonly hear men say: 'I must admit that in a sort of way it wasn't disagreeable.'† But in some way or another, almost everyone who was in England then speaks of those times as good: 'friendly', they will say, or 'neighbourly'. Some of the starch got washed out of bureaucracy as well as social relationships; ordinary people found themselves with responsibility, and found they could manage it perfectly well. We got a glimpse of the possibility of doing

* The Left Book Club, founded by Victor Gollancz in 1936, had fifty thousand members within a year.

† This from John Freeman, our ambassador in Washington from 1969–71. Note the double negative, avoiding a direct statement.

without 'Them'. Even during the war, the government itself admitted the shortcomings of the civil service: 'over-devotion to precedent, remoteness from the rest of the community, inaccessibility, and faulty handling of the general public ...' It was a list most of us could have compiled.

Even in 1942, before the war had reached its turning point, Harold Macmillan was saying that the British people were 'supremely prosperous and happy' and were it not for the bombing, would be perfectly content. But that does not tie up with the fact that, by that time, consumer spending had fallen by about a fifth since 1939. Over half the national income was being spent on the war—much more than in any other Allied nation except New Zealand. On the Home Front, though, there was an extraordinary spirit of unity. This, I imagine, is what Harold Macmillan really had in mind. War is the great leveller. There was so much that everyone shared, rich or poor—gas-masks, the Blackout, the same shortages, the same meat ration, the same chance of bomb damage, the same worry about relatives 'over there'. The same culture, even, seemed to be enjoyed by everyone: Tommy Handley in 'ITMA', and Myra Hess giving lunch-hour piano recitals in the National Gallery. Everyone had something to do, and all for the same purpose: Digging for Victory, frustrating the Squan-derbug, firewatching, Home Guard and A.R.P. (Air Raid Precautions) duty. Even Making Ends Meet in the circum-stances of war became part of the general effort. The W.V.S. (Women's Voluntary Services) gave the Women's Institute population something more to do than simply amuse them-selves: organizing the evacuation of children, mobile can-teens, emergency supplies, distributing clothing and 'Bundles for Britain' from the U.S.A. The W.V.S. got themselves a brilliant uniform that made every one of them look like a lady. They were happy to be so busy, to demon-strate how well the amateur could really get things done.

Our house was an Emergency Hospital, equipped with blankets and bandages in case of disaster. At one time, in 1940 I suppose, my mother drove almost daily to take evacuees to Victoria Station, sometimes passing men still working to clear the debris of the last night's raid.

The iron railings in front of our house were taken to be rendered into tanks. This happened everywhere, except where railings were needed for safety—there are very few London squares now with the railings intact. And there was a feeling that these small sacrifices made a real contribution. Though I doubt if everyone saw it as dramatically as the Western Daily Press:

> SMACK IN THE EYE FOR HITLER
> Burnham-on-Sea railings for scrap.

But the spirit of social unity was very largely dissipated after the war, and you have to be an old man now to remember the good old days of the Blitz. To become permanent a change had to be sufficiently desired by the whole community. Evidently it was not—despite the expectation of both extremes, those who desired it and those who dreaded it, that the 'old order had collapsed' (the words of Clement Attlee, in 1940, who desired it deeply), that 'the old world of privilege will disappear' (Harold Nicolson, five years later, who desired it morally, but feared he would stand to lose by it*), that the war, barring defeat, would wipe out most of the existing class privileges (according to George Orwell, 1941, who desired it with the emotional intensity of a man rejecting his own inheritance).

Now, thirty years after the second war, the old order certainly looks groggy. But it is too late to get back that

---

* His wife, on the other hand, somewhat guiltily admitted: 'I hate democracy. I hate *la populace*. I wish education had never been introduced. I don't like tyranny, but I like an intelligent oligarchy. I wish *la populace* had never been encouraged to emerge from its rightful place. I should like to see them as well-fed and well-housed as T.T. cows, but no more articulate than that.'

precious spirit of unity. The social change we are experiencing today is in the hands of men and women who were infants at the end of the war, if they were born at all. We, who were children during the war, should have kept its spirit going. But we grew up, and nothing happened. We were, indeed, the generation that did not show up.

For our family, the 1939–45 experience was on the Home Front. We had no close relatives in the Forces, so we did not follow the campaigns with flagged pins on the *Daily Telegraph* map of the world, like many others. None of us was old enough to be called up. My brother did have to go just at the end, but he very soon found himself a place as a driving instructor in the Artillery. The Watts's elder son was in the Gunners too, and not unexpectedly came out an officer—a captain or major, I suppose. My brother was a sergeant, and would not have wanted a commission. In those days they were socially evaluated. The Watts family were more socially adroit than ours. As far as we children were concerned, the fighting overseas was not quite real. The six and nine o'clock News were landmarks of the day, but it felt like someone else's war they were reporting, not ours.* For us, Macmillan could have been right. The war was an adventure. There was certainly no hunger, and only irritating shortages, like sweets and bananas, many of them mitigated by parental sacrifice.

Under months of air raids, even at the height of the Blitz, the assault was too diffuse for real fear, except at moments of actual bombing or, later, when the VIs—the Doodlebugs—chugged over like 400-mile-an-hour lawn-mowers and ran out of petrol overhead. The rest of the time the reaction was bravado, or the sort of cheeky Cockney humour London got a name for. Nevertheless, it was no joke in bombed areas. In two nights in 1941,

---

* The newsreaders identified themselves—'and this is Alvar Liddell reading it'—in order that we could be sure it was not a traitorous impostor. It was a comfort to hear the familiar names, but I never understood that reasoning.

two thousand five hundred people were killed in raids on London.

Instead of an air-raid shelter, my father fortified the kitchen. It was a single-storey addition at one end of the house. Thick concrete slabs were laid on the roof, and this was supported inside by three or four wooden pillars. Wooden shutters were made to fit on the outside of the windows, and heavy blackout curtains on the inside. There we children slept on camp beds, stumbling or being carried downstairs when the sirens sounded, or, when the raids were frequent, going to bed there in the first place. My mother and father moved their bed down to the drawing room. We were sometimes frightened then, with the guns cracking round like thunder. You could hear the emplacements opening up one after another. 'They're getting closer,' we would say. But my parents never showed fear, and that probably prevented us from being much afraid.

My father made regular rounds of the works and kept an eye open for incendiary bombs. Once a 'breadbasket' of them — seventy-two bombs, two pounds each — fell on the marsh over the road from the house, raining safely down like a huge firework display. A couple fell on our ground, one against a workshop door, one in the garden. They were small things, easily put out with a bucket of sand. But if my father had not been there, the wooden door of the workshop would certainly have caught fire.

Otherwise we were just far enough from London to miss heavy bombing. We guessed the Germans would make for the gunpowder factory, which doubtless was making explosives as fast as it could; but it was never hit. When the Blitz was at its height my mother took a room twenty miles away in the country, in the village where I was then at school. When we were at home for the holidays she drove us every night, my sister and me, out to the safety of the country. It must have been a strain, facing that drive on dark nights, with the lights taped to slits. On moonlit nights she did not have to go—the Luftwaffe only felt safe in cloudy weather. Ironically that village did get bombed. A solitary mine—a land-mine on a parachute—drifted out and landed in an oak tree in the fields not far from the house where we used to sleep. It may have blown out some windows, and scared the breath out of a few cattle, but it did no real harm.

From September 3rd to November 7th, 1940, London was raided every night. Daylight raids were rarer, but if you did catch sight of the planes the picture was unforgettable. I remember standing in our little concrete back yard (this must have been the summer of 1940), and watching the dog fights going on, right up there where the planes were like toys, silver on a blue board, drawing threads of cotton after them. You held your breath as you watched. When one of them fell away, smoking, to crash somewhere unseen, you strained your eyes to see whether it was theirs or ours. Once—the recollection is so vivid that I sometimes wonder if it was a dream—as I was standing under the two chestnut trees that grew in the river bank at the bottom of the paddock, a great plane dived at me from nowhere. There were thick ropes of dark smoke pouring from its tail. I could clearly see the black cross on its wings. It was so low it must have been about to crash. But it didn't. I waited for the explosion, and none came. The plane simply disappeared into thin air. But it was not a ghost; others saw it too. Local opinion had it that it was a reconnaissance plane, diving low to take photographs under pretence of crashing.

However, war was by no means all so ominous for us kids. We made collections: pieces of shrapnel, a burnt-out incendiary bomb, with its bitter, metallic smell. My brother had a special trophy: a lump of yellowish Perspex from the screen of a crashed plane. We learnt new expressions, from 'Got any gum, chum?' to 'Wizard prang!' And new songs. Naughtily we sang, to the tune of 'Colonel Bogey':

> Hitler has only got one ball.
> Goering has two, but very small.
> Himmler has something simmler.
> But Goebbels has noebbels at all.

Later in the war, when bombing was not so troublesome and nothing like so regular, we slept at home, in our own beds. But when the V1s occasionally came across, where you could see or hear them, that was frightening. You knew that if you could hear them you were probably safe, since they would glide on another mile after the engine cut out, but it was enough to make you put your head under the clothes.

Of the V2s, the giant rockets launched from Holland, there was no warning at all; they simply arrived, with a great bang (they carried a ton of explosive). Fortunately the Germans only got off one thousand three hundred before the bases were overrun. The sixth from last of those landed five hundred yards from our house, right in the middle of the road. It destroyed a number of houses and a pub, severed the mains and generally made a lot of mess. My mother had just come in, and taken the evening paper from the door. She walked to the dining-room window to catch the last of the light. The window fell in on her. But she was not hurt. And by some miracle not much damage was done to the house. We found large pieces of paving-stone stuck in the grass in the garden, and fragments about the place. But either the little hump-backed bridge between us and the rocket, or some chance pattern of shock-waves, saved both our house and the garage from anything more than cracked ceilings and broken glass.

In those times I guess I was no more or less happy because of the war. At the age of seven you have a very flexible idea of normality, especially when you have had the amazing experience of going away to boarding school.

The whole of adult life is mysterious. War seems just another change to adjust to.

The war stayed with us for so long that many of my wartime memories are post-war. I have a ration book still. I suppose it is the last. It is dated 1953–4, and the yellow coupons for meat, eggs, fats, cheese, bacon and sugar are cancelled with a 'Cambridge' stamp. That was after I had been in the army myself for two years. It's not surprising that I can't actually remember the end of the war. The things that meant war to us children went on. I suppose that at the time I was at school in Buckinghamshire, struggling with the Latin conditional under the eye of old Mr Evans. None of the younger masters had come back. The Land Girls went on strutting round in their breeches. We did not get any more sweets. When we went on holiday to Frinton, the beach was still protected with steel scaffolding to keep off the invasion barges. The poles were rusty from the spray and exposure, peeling in rough scales. Ignoring my mother's warning, I climbed and monkeyed on them and, as she predicted, slipped and grazed my thigh. I carry an almost imperceptible scar — my only war wound.

I have no experience of war, or even battle. I did once set out across the desert towards Cairo, expecting a small skirmish with an incompetent native force before riding in triumph in a tank through the city … but the affair was called off, before the excitement was cooled by the thought of facing real shells. Battle experience really divides the men from the boys. As time goes on without war, the division grows less obtrusive. But it's always lying in wait to attack that old-fashioned image of manhood. You can't criticize military methods unless you've been out there where there are men shooting at you, and aiming to kill. Even stout Dr Johnson: 'Every person thinks meanly of himself for not having been a soldier, for not having been to sea.' Two hundred years later Sir Harold Nicolson wrote to his sons, both serving in the war: 'It has been a dead weight on my life never to have known the dangers of the last war and never to have discovered whether I am a hero or a coward.' It is a common regret.

I am glad never to have had to test myself on a battle-field. But my later experience of the Forces makes me doubt whether the military experienced the shake-up we had at home—the social shake-up. Army discipline, and so much of its efficiency, depends on the superior/inferior relationship. Once you had the king's commission you were part of a segregated elite. Even prisoners of war were kept in separate camps: officers and other ranks. When I was first called up, even in basic training it was clear on what grounds this selection was made. Those of us who got through the War Office Selection Board—called 'Wosby'—and went back to camp before going off for officer training were told by the experienced privates, 'I knew you'd be going. You can always tell—the ones that wear pyjamas.' And he was right. Ordinary men slept in their underwear. The middle class wore pyjamas. The upper class wore nothing.

If I had been in the war I should probably have been an officer, since I was later, when not so many were required. It is quite likely, too, that I should not have survived: junior Artillery officers, directing the fire of their guns from some convenient lookout, far ahead, were notoriously short-lived. My brother had advised me to join the Gunners. His reason was simple: the infantry were always marching about, but in the Gunners you rode everywhere. Later, scudding about the Egyptian desert with a battery of tank-mounted guns, raising a small sandstorm, it was amusing to think that that was the reason I was there. I had taken trouble with my laziness: at school I volunteered for the Artillery section of the Junior Training Corps—scorned by the main force—to make sure I got into the Gunners for National Service. I doubt if it made any difference.

Corps training was compulsory at school, one afternoon a week and occasional exercises. I never enjoyed it. I did not inherit from my mother her neat way with a uniform. Whenever I got into mine, then or later, I was conscious that my body was the wrong shape to carry it off. On other people the thick material hung in sharp creases; on me it was stiff and intractable, bulging like a corn sack. Even my beret, which should have fallen smoothly to one side, stuck out rigidly in every wrong direction. I never did get head-gear right, until I abandoned it altogether.

The Junior Training Corps had, until recently before, been known as the Officer Training Corps; and despite the change of name this was what it was still intended for. More correctly, I suppose, the public-school training anyway made it more likely that those who went through J.T.C. there would get to be officers. After boarding school the style of life was familiar, if not enjoyable. I do not think it occurred to me once that it would be anything but disastrous not to become an officer. Like failing an exam, something to be ashamed of. Everyone told me so, either directly or implicit-ly. I never came in contact with other opinion. I am sure all the masters at school had been officers — if, in some cases, only just. At the W.O.S.B. we were divided into groups of about ten, and put through a couple of days of physical initiative tests and discussion groups, closely watched all the time by men with clip-boards. Here again I remember the familiar feeling of muted panic. For the first six months in the Army I woke every morning in panic. I never quite got on top of it. It was the same later. I never quite got on top of classics. I never quite got on top of Law.

Murderous assault courses and sadistic sergeant-majors: the horrors of the officer-training course were legendary. But it was more myth than legend. The assault course was not too taxing, even for me. Famous R.S.M. Brittain, with his pace stick* tucked firmly under his arm, screamed at us

---

* Like giant dividers, the pace stick measures whether you are marching with steps the correct length. It's a pretty sight to see a sergeant-major (less massive than R.S.M. Brittain) beside a quick-marching unit, stylishly twisting the pace stick from point to point across the parade ground.

like an agonized walrus from the other side of the parade ground, and told us we marched like pregnant nuns. When he shouted an order it seemed as if he was trying to take off, to rise from the ground, but was stuck; there was movement at his knees and thighs, and the fat on his neck, which he had shorn almost naked, quivered terribly. But nothing terrible happened. The Army was like school, with the screws tightened. Some things were actually the same: both favoured cross-country runs, that mobile torture.

At the end of the course Major Singleton did his best to persuade some of us to volunteer for a regiment of airborne gunners. 'Damn good fun,' he said, with that eager clenching of the jaw. 'Started the training m'self. But I broke a leg.' I was coward enough already, without that encouragement. I had joined the Gunners to avoid walking; falling perhaps required less energy still, but obviously it had other disadvantages.

Instead I was posted to Germany to the second senior regiment in the Artillery.* They may not have been the Coldstream, but they were an elite, and they knew it. You can almost smell a good regiment: it gives off the scent of arrogant efficiency. Regimental loyalty is fierce. The sergeants walk about like stags, spoiling for a fight. Every man's uniform is tailored to fit. Reflexes and creases, both are sharp as razors.

By chance I was only in Germany two or three months. In time I might have felt at home, but as it was I felt distinctly out of place. Much of this was social discomfort — that, combined with a very sketchy knowledge of the practice of artillery warfare. Almost immediately on my arrival the whole regiment set out on a prolonged exercise. I

---

* Third, if you include the King's Troop, R.H.A., who maintain the old horse-drawn gun carriages, with which they give displays and fire ceremonial salutes. There are five regiments of Royal Horse Artillery. After them come the field regiments —'Royal Artillery', plain. The senior of these (starting with 6th Field), however, had still S.P. (self-propelled) 25-pounder guns, mounted on a tank chassis—the modern equivalent of horse artillery. Common field regiments have towed guns. With S.P. guns, naturally, there is even less footwork.

believe we were practising a delayed withdrawal—this was in 1952—should the Russians take the initiative and invade from the East. I was appointed Assistant Command Post Officer of one battery (there are three in a regiment). It very soon became clear that the duties of ac/C.P.O. had been no more than glossed over at OCTU (Officer Cadet Training Unit). My C.P.O., Sebag-Montefiore, enclosed in the command post—a metal box on tracks, a tank crossed with a caravan—expended amazing energy on a feverish personal battle with his equipment—never less than two sets of headphones and a telephone line to the guns. He wrestled these with a passionate intensity. They seemed always on the point of failure. The headphones relayed faint, indistinct signals that were all we knew of essential map references. By sheer force of will, repeating and verifying these numbers in a particular high-pitched shout he had perfected to carry on the air, Sebag-Montefiore invariably won this battle with imminent breakdown, but by quite a narrow margin. I watched him in helpless admiration.

Soon afterwards I was transferred to another regiment. It was a typical military charade. Those regiments, as you would expect, were jealous of their seniority. In the R.H.A. the batteries were called 'troops', and these were named after their original and famous commanders. It happened that, in the confusion of war, and the re-forming of scattered units, Bull's Troop had jumped seniority. There were batteries in *field* regiments more senior, it seemed. Unfortunately, the regiment in which Bull's Troop belonged by seniority was in Egypt. There could not be any question of changing the entire personnel. Indeed, the present members had been trained by, and were loyal to, their R.H.A. image; they would not want to be 'demoted'. It was therefore decided to send out a cadre to represent the troop. I was seconded to Bull's Troop specially to take it away to its rightful place. They did seem indecently keen to get rid of me. With three men and six crates of battery silver—

candlesticks and other decorations for the Mess tables – I
went back to Woolwich and then, by boat, calling at Algiers
and Famagusta, to the Great Bitter Lake.

Somewhere in those crates were the volumes of 'battery
history' of Bull's Troop, the record of their service over
more than a hundred years. I doubt if I should have known
much of it if I had been with them from the start; as it was,
I knew nothing. And when I arrived in Egypt, a parade of
the new Bull's Troop had been called for the next day: I
was to lecture them on battery history. When I explained
the position, I was given a fortnight to learn it.

In 1952 the Egyptians were trying to get us out of the
Canal Zone. They had signed a treaty giving us a base there
until 1956, but they wanted to end it then and there. We
were virtually a besieged garrison. Cairo, Alexandria, Petra,
were within travelling distance, but they were all out of
bounds. We could go to Ismailia, but only the main streets
there were thought safe. There are ways in which trouble
can be felt quite far down the military scale. Married quar-
ters were being closed and wives sent home. The burden of
night guard duties began to disrupt the pattern of training.
We found ourselves on unusual duties – unloading ships,
for instance. Rumours circulated: a man knifed in Ismailia,
a raid at a pumping station. If you saw a civilian in the desert
outside the camp you told the guards and they kept an eye
on him. Civilian workers in the camp, the barber, the laun-
dry men, the bootmaker, had their passes doublechecked.

Much of our time was spent guarding strategic points –
the perimeter of the camp, fuel dumps, and generating and
freshwater pumping stations. (The 'Sweetwater Canal' was
so named in contrast to the salt Bitter Lakes. It was not to
be taken literally – I have myself seen a dead camel in it.)

The garrison petrol dump was remote and eerily silent.
On guard duty in the night, the officer, the sergeant and
two men toured the outside of the wire in the Land-
Rover every two or three hours, sweeping the rough desert

ground with a searchlight for signs of guerrilla activity. Out there a pack of pi-dogs ran like wolves. As I remember it, they were of various types, but all large. They pursued the open Land-Rover, and easily kept pace with it — on the rough ground you could not make much speed. We did not shoot the dogs, since it was reckoned they would give us warning of any approach from outside. But as they bounded along beside us, snapping at our legs and snarling, the guard sergeant would lean out and hit them on the head with the butt of a sten. Under my Sam Browne my heart was beating wildly — more from terror than excitement.

In 1954 the government decided to withdraw their eighty thousand troops from the Canal Zone. In the House of Commons, Captain Waterhouse declared that the country was becoming weary of responsibility. 'Our burdens are becoming too heavy for us,' he said, 'and we are losing our will to rule.' He went off to live in Rhodesia, where the order of things was more as he understood it. Churchill referred to the withdrawal as the 'scuttle' of the base, but Anthony Eden assured him that President Nasser was to be trusted.

Two years later Nasser nationalized the Suez Canal. British reaction was hysterical. It was exactly what Colonel Blimp — John Bull, but, significantly, twenty years older and quite evidently ridiculous — had predicted all along. How often had he said it: Never trust the wogs? Anthony Eden, then Prime Minister (though the incident was to bring him down), began to think he had been deceived in trusting Nasser by a desire to do the modern thing, and that actually Colonel Blimp was right. He had been betrayed. The moral righteousness of British Late Empire rose from its death-bed, shaking with rage. Britain had always known that the natives laughed at her behind her back: let them laugh, she had comforted herself, as long as they also feared her. Actual insubordination she had always suppressed with ruthless promptitude. One of the first rules of a nation that controlled a quarter of the world's population, as Britain did at the beginning of the century — a quarter of a million soldiers containing 500 million people — was not to allow them to get away with anything. As it was originally, the gunboat mentality was only the prudent way to control such vast numbers, so widely spread.

By 1956 the British were emerging from the debris of the war and beginning to look round. They finally began to realize that the old international order no longer existed. Many of them had been fighting with the vague idea that this was what they were preserving. And now it seemed that the whole world expected the British to stand by and allow the *Egyptians* to defy them. It was shattering. Harold Macmillan mentioned the end of civilization; Anthony Eden, the 'ignoble end to our long history'. Everyone recalled the humiliation of appeasement in the 'thirties, equating Nasser with Hitler. The memory of Chamberlain holding up that piece of paper, after his final meeting with Hitler, and speaking of 'peace in our time', was bitter and humiliating. To many it still is.

And in the event, Suez was in a way the more humiliating. The greatest powers can suffer betrayal. And, after all, we can say we took our revenge on Hitler for that. But to be ordered to cease operations by your bank manager, an American, and having to take notice of him, is plain evidence that you no longer call the shots. You can try to bluff it out: 'We do of course live in a rather difficult time,' said Harold Macmillan, with his natural mastery of the English idiom, 'but we have done that before. At the moment we seem rather isolated, but we have been that before. Nothing matters as long as we think what we have done is right.'

But whatever we say, we have at last learnt our lesson. There have been times when it has seemed we might commit one final folly of the Suez type, in Cyprus (where the Suez base moved), or Malta, or Gibraltar or the West Indies. Old habits die hard. We still take up paternal attitudes whenever there is trouble overseas, particularly in

Africa, as if by right we are the Solomon of the world. What we cannot accept is that not having a role is a creditable and desirable position.

The imperial role was anyway something we had invented for our own purposes. Trade had merged into conquest, with a typical fudging of the demarcation. In the nineteenth century we began to get heavy ideas; we began to develop a public conscience. The difficulty is that, once you admit the equality of man, you have to be careful how you take advantage of him. The Victorians, with a combination of 'high-minded naïvety and ruthless egoism', in the period of Late Empire began to patronize the native. They had turned empire into a duty. They became obsessed with it. It affected the whole fabric of society: 'To keep the Empire,' said Winston Churchill in 1899, 'we must have Imperial stock ... To keep our Empire we must have a free people and an educated people and a well-fed people. This is why we are in favour of social reform.' It is, of course, the British people whose freedom has to be protected. H. G. Wells sums up his attitude at about this time, when he was thirteen, 'We English, by sheer native superiority, practically without trying, had possessed ourselves of an empire on which the sun never set, and through the errors and infirmities of other races were being forced slowly but steadily and quite modestly—towards world dominion.'

One of the things that rankled about the disaster of Suez was that we knew the Egyptians were cowards. In a straight fight we should have run them into the desert like jackals from the British lion. We pride ourselves—used to pride ourselves—on our courage in battle. And that courage we maintained by discipline. Discipline again involves role-playing. At the age of eighteen, swagger-cane in hand, conscious of my inelegant headgear, and the fact that I was overweight, I was ordering round forty-year-old sergeants who had fought through the war and knew more of gunnery than I ever should. But they also knew that the structure of the Services depended on this role-playing. They would tactfully cover my mistakes, not because they cared for my comfort, but because they were trained to protect the system, and the system ran on obedience. In the long run, but near enough to see it as reality, their own life might depend on it. Like everything that happens before your own experience I thought of the war in those days as something that happened way in the past. Yet it had ended only seven years before. No wonder the regulars in Germany treated civilian property so carelessly. I had been brought up to respect property, and I hesitated to site guns on growing crops, or a command post in a farmyard. They impatiently pointed out that the umpires followed round and fixed compensation, and we were intended to carry out this exercise as if we meant it. It was not so long ago that they were fighting over this country, and the farmers were the enemy.

The Other Ranks had been trained to obedience. It took a hundred years of social indoctrination to make possible the appalling misery of the trench warfare of World War I, and then at times it was a near thing. The officers had been trained to confuse game with reality, and to play games more seriously than life. They took to the battlefield, or the military exercise, in the same spirit of keenness as they took to the rugger field.

This is the British military tradition. It works as a reflection of civilian society. The pink-cheeked young squire — many families had the tradition of military service by which the younger sons became professional soldiers and even the eldest would do service while awaiting their inheritance — would be taken over by the experienced sergeant and taught how to play the game, just as the head gamekeeper would have taught him to shoot, or the head groom to ride. We fought well not because of our well-trained Army — we scarcely had a standing army — but because we had a well-trained society. Wellington called his men 'the scum of the earth'. The officers were inclined to treat Army life as a convenient frame for a continuing social life, and for the socially ambitious it was a chance to get in with the best society. As we had a hundred years of peace in the nineteenth century, and have never been properly invaded since 1066, you would scarcely expect a strong military tradition, or for it to have changed very sharply.

The old forms were still being acted out in my time. The R.H.A. regiment in the elegant ex-Luftwaffe barracks may have been an exception; but in Egypt the amenities included the regimental polo ground (I believe only one of our officers was wealthy enough to keep his own ponies), sailing from the Officers' Club in Fayid on the Bitter Lake, and tennis on the court at the Officers' Mess (a mixture of Nile mud and sand made a passable hard court). There were parties down at the Club, where the proportion of men to women was ten to one and the only diversion was to get helplessly drunk. Your batman called you in the morning with shaving-water and a clean belt, newly blancoed, with polished brasses, and you woke to that strange unmistakable smell of the East—not spicy and exotic, but sterile and musty, the smell of ancient, stale sand. Once smelt, you never forget it.

> If you've 'eard the East a-callin'
> You won't ever 'eed aught else,

Kipling wrote in 'Mandalay', in that literary Cockney that seems so patronizing now. But now neither the social structure nor the methods of warfare require that sort of army. If we ever have to fight again, the whole arrangement will be different. We have been able to watch a highly mechanized, democratic army at work in Vietnam, and it is not like anything we have ever known.

One reason for the *ad hoc* nature of the old Army lay in the reliability of the Navy. Being the instrument of exploration and of trade, our ships could be said to have started it all. And now we have a rather misty-eyed view of the Senior Service.

Socially it has been a snob service – though it probably attracted less of the aristocracy than the Army – and princes seem to prefer to get married in naval uniform. That's one reason, though it might have been subconscious, that a Labour government sought to disband a great part of it. Hearts of Oak, Jack Tar, 'Rule Britannia',* the Singeing of the King of Spain's Beard, Drake at his bowls, England Expects ... this naval folklore gives a swaggering picture of what in those days was actually a press-ganged force, brutally disciplined. The Navy has always been our national punitive force, in control of every ocean of the world. It did not bother to give itself a national name: the Royal Navy has always been the British Navy, no matter what waters it sailed in. The view from the shore – and no part of Britain is more than seventy miles from the sea – is comforting, and at that distance it is easy to overlook the unfortunate aspects. We have always trusted the Navy. It was rarely situated where it could take advantage of its power and threaten to take over government. No need to fear a naval coup.

Naval ships are being laid up, or scrapped; our docks are closing; our shipyards face bankruptcy. But we still have the sense of a naval tradition. Still Cunard Lines can say, 'It will be a national disaster if the QE2 turbines were to fail again on the high seas after the ship entered service.'

* James Thomson, author of that rousing shanty, was himself notoriously idle. Lady Hertford, his patroness, records coming across him in her kitchen garden, eating a peach as it hung from the branch, not bothering to take his hand from his pocket. The matriarchial figure of Britannia first appeared on our coinage in 1672.

8. *A State of Mediocrity*

There is one general grievance in the nation:
it is the law.

> Oliver Cromwell, 1656

I have often thought that our state here in this world is a state of mediocrity, which is not capable of extremes.

> John Locke, 1678

'Tis my opinion the Moderate Men of both Partyes are the Substantial part of a Nation. They are its refuge when the Men of Heat Carry Things too far.

> Daniel Defoe, 1704

How I love the English daring! How I love people who say what they think.

> Voltaire, 1759

Britain is the land of the amateur, the home of a famous compromise, of the 'good sport', of tolerance, of the art of diplomacy, of a widely imitated legal system. There is a family connection between these traits.

The amateur status is non-committal. It does not have to be taken too seriously. You can back out when you want. You have not put up a sign. If you treat it all as a game the choice remains with you whether to take it seriously or not. Our sportsmen have always made the point of being amateur. All artists we treat as amateurs. We like amateur theatricals, amateur detectives in our fiction. In real life too, we would get Det. Sup. Bert Smith C.I.D. on our case, but we should far prefer Sherlock Holmes or Lord Peter Wimsey. That is what an English gentleman is, an amateur who, being quite disinterested, can have no vulgar motives.

Our geography produces mists and grey skies, pale sunlight and modest flowers. We do not see things by harsh light, in black and white, but in grey shades. Whatever the subject, we are able to notice the shades of qualification, of implication. Being able to appreciate both sides, we lack the ability for enthusiasm. So we are non-committal, middle-of-the-road. Compromise therefore comes naturally —the diplomatic art. Look at it another way and it is evasiveness. We can seem to have a very fluid way with the truth, a shifting sense of actuality that turns out very like dishonesty.

Yet we are practical, and practicality deals in hard edges, in action and fact. We are anti-intellectual. Our first reaction to art is in practical terms: how nearly could I do as well as that myself? The idea counts for very little. We like things handmade, and there is a snobbery about slightly wonky pottery and uneven hand-knitting. We like it because it is imperfect, it looks amateur, and it is pretty certain we could do as well ourselves if we just gave it the time. We are a nation of self-helpers. For so long we have expected that the machinery and the expertise were only a matter of common sense. Since our avowed professionals so often turn out no more than amateur, self-help becomes necessary. We are clean, and we spend money reluctantly. So a great Do-It-Yourself industry has sprung up to service those who want to tinker with their cars, cure dripping taps, tile round the bath, install an extractor fan in the kitchen, panel the dining-room, build a slate fireplace.

This amateurism has long been the style of our enterprises. Offhandedly we have claimed that we 'muddle through'. Results show that in some cases we have been able to muddle through with deadly efficiency. But we enjoy the joke that it is all a rather charming accident. We are not at all concerned that we might be thought lazy or incompetent. Our caring what people think does not extend very far. It is the neighbours that matter; we don't give a fig for what they think of us across the Channel.

Our diplomats, politicians, even our businessmen, have been playing such a game for years. Casual, languid, frivolous—they would sooner be thought anything other than professional. 'I have no idea where the Virgin Islands are,' says the senior Foreign Office official, 'but I assume they must be some way from the Isle of Man.' It is an important part of the English style. Harold Macmillan played the amateur with a high professional skill. He would dismiss problems with vague expressions of confidence: 'Oh, everyone will rally round when the time comes.' He spoke of politics as 'fun'. When Chancellor of the Exchequer he made a point of arriving calmly rather late for Cabinet meetings from his house next door. As Prime Minister he tried to give the impression that, after a hard day bagging grouse, he sat at the fire reading Trollope and sorted out the country's problems by a chat on the phone with his good friend Dwight Eisenhower over there. 'He has charm,' reads an early report on him as an M.P., 'marred perhaps by a touch of smugness. Smugness, however, with him is free from the slightest taint of insincerity.' Yet the most commonly mentioned aspect of his nature was his duality, his ambiguity, his gift for simulation. He had a great sympathy for the deprived, but he was most at home with the privileged. He was relaxed, but sharp. Now tough, now romantic. Behind the manner of an 'unflappable' 'Edwardian' gentleman, son-in-law of a duke, on whose lips hopefully modern phrases — 'You never had it so good', for instance — seemed so out of place, was a professional politician, with a passion for organization, a keen brain and a total grasp of the science of economics.

It is a game we play very well, modestly brushing aside praise that we know we deserve. Sometimes the game takes over, turning us into spies, or dare-devils, in which parts we have played with distinction. Under American influence, this style is pretty much out of fashion now. The newer game is apparent professionalism. It's still the appearance that counts. It remains a game, but now it has to be played with a serious expression.

Our tendency to compromise, reconciling as it does the ability to see every side of the question, has made us a tolerant nation, with a great respect for fair play. 'For really I think that the poorest he that is in England', said Leveller Colonel Rainborough, in the Putney debates with Cromwell's officers in 1647, 'hath a life to live, as the greatest he; and therefore truly, sir, I think it's clear, that every man that is to live under a government ought first by his own consent to put himself under that government ... I should doubt whether he was an Englishman or no, that should doubt of these things.' We even tolerate Communist candidates in elections, treating them merely as political eccentrics.

The compromise, the amateurism, that soft bluish haze that blurs the outline of our landscape, have in recent history made Britain a bland country, the refuge of good taste. Houses are painted cream — neither white nor a colour, and a most practical shade. The usual compliment is that 'it's very nice'. As long as it's not too ... It makes for a most relaxing atmosphere, and foreigners find it a pleasant country to visit. The young revolt with their own style, but to most of them compromise is an inherited characteristic, and they make muted protest, a polite revolution, of which time is the chief weapon, and the outcome uncertain.

Not wishing to cause trouble, and being such ardent gamesmen, convinced by the doctrine of fair play, we are a law-abiding nation, ready to live according to the rules. Most Englishmen believe that, by and large, justice is done. We even believe that the inevitable occasional 'unfairness' of the strict letter of the law will be tempered by the humanity of our judges. Equity will prevail over law, and right will triumph. It's out of fashion in the world now for visiting starlets to tell us our policemen are wonderful — but we know it without being reminded. TV serials say it all the time by implication. The judiciary has evidently done a good job of getting justice 'seen to be done'. Judges seem purposely to present themselves as old-fashioned and unworldly, protectors of an ancient morality. Recently a twenty-five-year-old man came before a judge, claiming damages for injury in an accident. His counsel claimed that his sex-life had suffered. 'Is he married?' asked the judge. 'No.' 'Then I don't see how his life can have changed.' Yet somehow that seems endearing and appropriate. The law takes the place of the Church, fighting a rearguard action against modernity, testing its quality lest it take over too quickly.

'The law is a ass — a idiot,' said Mr Bumble in *Oliver Twist*, and we frequently quote him. We speak resignedly of 'the Law's delay' (this is Hamlet's phrase), but we are never so seriously discontented that we plan to challenge its authority. We have a practical approach,* and we esteem facts, so that the dry, apparently factual legal manner is very much to our taste. The law resolves mysteries, to our relief: it is not in our temperament to enjoy what has not been resolved.

I got into the law, not by design, but by the elimination of the alternatives. At times of stress I still have a recurring nightmare: I am about to go back to Cambridge for my last term, and at the end of this I shall have to take a final exam, which I know I shall not pass. I have realized I am wasting my time at university, and ought to drop out. But perhaps I only think I want to drop out to avoid taking that impossible exam? Actually I *know* I ought to drop out, but what would people think? That's the colour of my courage to face the exam, the fear of being seen to be afraid.

The dream combines several pieces of the past, but it is basically accurate. I switched from classics to law for no positive reason. I began to think that law might be a satisfactory career. The fathers of several of my friends were in the law—it is the ultimate middle-class profession. It had the respectability and the stability that I knew would comfort my parents. And my own impetus in other directions was too feeble to take me any distance. The man at the Appointments Board glanced at my first choice—publishing —and passed without a word to my second—solicitor. I had not even had the sense to discover that every second undergraduate thinks that a life as a publisher's editor would suit him very well.

Like almost everything in Britain, the law has been bedevilled by class. In the first place the division between

---

* I once served as juror for a London Quarter Sessions. About a hundred of us reported to the Law Courts at the Elephant and Castle. After we had been separated into groups, the usher took us to our room to explain the procedures. Before he began—the death penalty was in force at this time, but much debated—he asked, 'No one here, is there, has any funny ideas about capital punishment?'

barristers and solicitors was a class division: barristers were employed by the well-to-do to plead their case, in questions of property, and for that they preferred counsel of their own type. Since then barristers have done what they can to preserve their position. Their whole manner infers that they consider themselves superior to solicitors. Though quite a number of students pass the Bar exams, many go straight into industry or the City, many are foreigners who return home, and only a small percentage are called to the Bar. Starting at the Bar meant, when I was a lawyer, a year in barrister's chambers, as a pupil, and an indefinite time waiting for briefs: in other words, the need for some independent income to tide over hard times.

There are now about two thousand practising barristers. A barrister cannot be briefed by a client direct: it has to be arranged by a solicitor. The law is often accused of inventing procedure to the benefit of its own purse, and that looks suspiciously the case here. The Bar argues that the system is a protection for the impartiality of justice. Counsel pleads on the legal merits of the case, and justice prevails. This is a quite naïve proposal, and evidently untrue. No one would stump up the enormous fees of legal representation in order that his own advantage be sacrificed to the sanctity of the law. If litigants can be so unselfish it would be better if all judgments were made by tribunal. What the system actually creates is a device by which counsel can tell a lie without getting the smell of it on his hands. 'Is that really so, Mr Smith?' the judge asks counsel incredulously. 'That is what I am instructed, m'lud.' His hands are clean, his probity immaculate. It seems his client (whom he met for the first time half an hour before, outside the court — they shook hands and spoke enough for counsel to assess his quality as a witness) has from birth, on sudden unpredictable occasions, of which this unfortunate incident happened to be one, confused black with white. That is what counsel has been instructed. He himself is telling the truth. He would not condone a lie. The judge draws his own conclusions as to the veracity of the client.

But this is an elaborate game. Solicitors write their instructions to counsel, setting out the basis of the case, with half a mind already on the lines on which counsel will plead. Together they have a conference to discuss their tactics. Solicitors are less delicate than counsel, or are said to be, and they might even suggest to a client that there are useful facts he may have 'forgotten'. But counsel play the same game, more fastidiously. I have been at conference with counsel where he has suggested, 'If your client were prepared to say ...' This is not simply, as it might sound, a matter of lies and truth. When counsel says, 'If your client were prepared to say ...' he does not draw a convenient lie out of the air. He is referring to something that has been introduced in the brief, or during discussion, and suggesting that it might be taken just so much further, that it might be refined to the point where the client could make this convenient statement.

What the law encourages is a version of the English lie. This is a native method of lying without telling an actual untruth. *Have you slept with her?* 'How dare you accuse me of such a thing!' *Have you slept with her?* 'She's really not my type.' *Have you slept with her?* 'I refuse to answer that question.' These answers are perfectly deceitful, but they seem to satisfy a sense of propriety that would be offended by a direct lie. It is another clue to the insoluble puzzle of British ambiguity.

The relationship between judge and counsel might be to the benefit of justice, but it is also a relationship of comrades. Only barristers may plead in the higher courts. Two thousand is a small-enough body for almost all of them to be known to the judges — especially as they usually specialize, and appear repeatedly in the same courts, before the same judges. But more important, it is from the ranks of barristers only that judicial appointments are made. There are at least four hundred permanent posts, and many more temporary or deputy ones. As Lord Goodman — a solicitor — has written: 'A young man of reasonable ability registering entry at the Bar today is engaged almost in a process of self-selection for some form of judgeship.'

Against two thousand barristers, in rough figures, we can compare a figure of twenty thousand solicitors. But even this is not a wide-open profession. Every solicitor has to serve at least three years as an articled clerk in a legal office. The average wage of articled clerks is seven pounds or so a week, and the work leaves little time for moonlighting. To exist at all requires some supplement.

Fifteen years ago I was paid three pounds a week. But this was an exception. Many firms still required the clerk himself to pay a premium. The Appointments Board sent me to a grand old firm in Bedford Square, where piles of deed-boxes stood about like coffins. (You used to be able to tell a lot about the *class* of a firm of solicitors by the number of those black tin boxes, each painted with the name of the client.) The partner's office I was shown into was attractively Dickensian, with leather chairs and an open coal fire. He mentioned two hundred and fifty pounds for the burden of having me about for three years. Even those firms that waived a premium rarely paid a salary.

I had been glad while I was at Cambridge that I had changed to law. Academically I found it enjoyable. It has something of the crossword quality of the classics, but with a sense of real life. It was, however, the mental exercise, not the social relevance, that made it enjoyable. It was just sufficiently difficult to stretch my mind. That's not to say I ever mastered it easily: faced with the rituals of conveyancing, even with the simple logic of its processes, my mind was thrown into panic and confusion.

The categories of civil law demonstrate a whole social history. New liabilities can arise to deal with new conditions, or new attitudes. 'The categories of negligence are never closed,' said Lord Macmillan in the House of Lords, in the case of *Donoghue v. Stevenson* in 1932. A woman had found a dead snail in her bottle of ginger-beer. After much argument it was held that the manufacturing company had a liability direct to her, since they must expect an eventual consumer of their product, to whom they owe a duty of care. This is the doctrine of fair play at work.

In this way, [said Lord Atkin, in the same case] rules of law arise which limit the range of complainants and the extent of their remedy. The rule that you are to love your neighbour becomes in law, you must not injure your neighbour; and the lawyer's question, Who is my neighbour? receives a restricted reply. You must take reasonable care to avoid acts or omissions which you can reasonably foresee would be likely to injure your neighbour. Who, then, in law is my neighbour? The answer seems to be—persons who are so closely and directly affected by my act that I ought reasonably to have them in contemplation when I am directing my mind to the acts or omissions which are called in question.

However, 'the duty does not extend beyond people of ordinary health or susceptibility,' explains Salmond's classic textbook on torts.

This was clearly laid down [it adds] in the House of Lords in *Bourhill v. Young* (e). There A, a motorcyclist, while driving at an excessive speed, collided with a motor-car and was killed. A fish-wife, whilst getting her fish-basket off the far side of a stationary tramcar, heard though she did not see the accident. Though she had no reasonable fear for immediate bodily injury to herself, she suffered from fright and was unable to carry on her business for some time. She was eight months pregnant and a month later the child was stillborn. It was held that she was not within the area of potential danger and the cyclist therefore owed no duty to her. (f)

(e)/1943/A.C. 92. The conclusion in this case has been criticised by Charlesworth, *Bourhill v. Young* (1943) L.Q.R. 150. See, however, Goodhart, *Bourhill v. Young* (1944) 8 Camb. L. J. 265.

(f) *Cf Pritchard v. Post Office*/1950/W.N. 310 (blind man); *Nova Mink, Ltd. v. Trans-Canada Airlines*/ 1951/2 D.L.R. 241 (noise of aeroplane causing female mink to devour young: no reason for pilot 'to envisage the presence of noise-conscious mink'). Yet see Prosser, s. 36; Paton, Text-book of Jurisprudence, 379.

Either your brain enjoys this sort of finessing, or you have no patience with it. It suited me very well. As a subject for study it has a lot of interest. But it has little to do with legal practice. The solicitor's client who is up there at the frontier of the law is rare indeed. As a rule, clients' problems fit into the established categories, and if they do not they are best forgotten. And if the client is adventurous, or of necessity gets into uncertain areas, the first thing the prudent solicitor will do is persuade him to pay for an opinion from leading counsel.

I was articled to my father's Number One solicitor. He had a Number Two man he employed for collecting debts and sorting out traffic offences. But for weighty matters, like making a will, or incorporating his company, he went to Mr Letts, in the City. I do not know the history of his arrangement for me to go there, but I guess it had some Masonic connection, through Mr Haylock. My father was a Mason, but only rarely attended meetings. His father, from The Green Man, had founded a Lodge (No. 4161: I have the gold fob watch* they gave him to commemorate

---

* A half hunter: that is, a watch with a hinged cover to protect the glass on the hunting field. A half hunter opens on the face side only; a hunter has a cover front and back.

the fact) and my father's membership was something honorary. Mr Haylock, though, was active in Masonry, was I believe Master of his Lodge, and gave initiates secret instruction in Masonic lore one or two nights a week.

Now Mrs Sweetenham's brother-in-law was a successful solicitor in Huddersfield, a man, I understood, of wealth and position. When he came to dinner, as he did once or twice when he was in the south, he was served on the best china. Mr Eaton-Smith was a collector of antiques, and his comments on our new heirlooms were remembered and sorted through afterwards for their full significance. He was a man given to extravagant compliments. He was also a good talker, a raconteur who dominated the dining-table — though at our table there would have been little competition. One night he told us about a client who had been involved in a road accident. He'd been drinking, and was somehow in collision with a car on the wrong side of the road. No one was hurt, but for some reason it was important that the client not be found guilty of the offence. Perhaps his licence was already endorsed, or he was a man in a public position. Mr Eaton-Smith made him repeat his story in precise detail. When he had finished, Mr Eaton-Smith said, 'But haven't you forgotten the little dog?' 'What little dog?' 'The little dog that ran out, that you swerved to avoid.'

I was very slow in getting the point of this story. I asked questions like, 'But was there *actually* a little dog?' Even for twenty-three, this displays a startling naïvety. My parents looked at me uncomfortably. They had been hoping Mr Eaton-Smith would make some complimentary comment about me, as well as about the china and the food — preferably that I was a genuine, natural, bound-to-succeed solicitor. But he did not. Only later it came back to my parents, and later still to me, that he had remarked to Mrs Sweetenham that I really was not cut out to be a solicitor at all.

In that he was right. But it took me some time to discover

it for myself. For eighteen months I set out daily to catch the train to London, carrying a tightly rolled umbrella and wearing a discreetly furry bowler, from Locks, and a *serious* expression. This was the City uniform (though recently the bowler has gone out of fashion). I took trouble to roll the umbrella thin as a cane. Those petty things were important: a silk umbrella that would roll neatly, a suit made-to-measure with cuffs that actually unbuttoned.

Mr Letts had warned me that he would not have time to instruct me himself; it was a condition of his taking me on. But not only did he not instruct me, his whole life was a mystery to me. When he was in the office he sat behind a large, empty desk. He smoked cigars and drank small cups of black coffee. The reference books—volumes of precedents, the Law Reports—were kept in his room and I had to check with his secretary that he was out before I could get the volumes I needed. Occasionally he would call for me and ask me to look something up for him, handing me the file from rather elegant, manicured hands. Once or twice I went with him to conference with counsel; otherwise I had no idea of what he was doing.

He was a director of a large store, solicitor to an insurance company, and expert on the intricacies of commercial-vehicle licensing. I did not feel he lacked sympathy for me, but I felt that he was a man who needed privacy, secrecy even, and was not in a hurry to make friends. No doubt he was a most discreet solicitor. I had the sense of a man who had made good over some fairly tough ground and had learnt the habit of moving carefully and letting the other man talk first. The office had a small department—two men and secretaries—working full time on vehicle licensing; I guess it was this connection that accounted for my being there. Mr Letts himself appeared only occasionally before the licensing board. (There was no question of barristers only in that procedure.) Reputedly he had once stalked that legal jungle like a tiger. But you would not have guessed it when I knew him. He sat silently at his desk, in a suit of expensive silver-grey material, very slightly sinister, as if waiting for prey.

The office was a serious place, drably furnished. No one seemed to enjoy what they were doing. I suppose clients in the waiting-room might be put off by gales of dirty laughter from the probate clerk, but it was not so much riotous fun that was missing as any sense of vitality. In the secretaries' room there was a heady smell of women, and the sexual exchange was going on all the time, of course, but in a somehow seedy fashion. There were the usual office stories of people coming back for forgotten keys and finding X giving it to Y on the table in the accounts office. One of the men dictated with his hand up his secretary's skirt. It was pretty well common knowledge. They seemed to have got into this habit. If you ever went into the room, she would be standing behind the desk beside him, while he explained some form she had to get completed. According to him it never went further than that. Sex apart, it was such a lifeless office, smelling of dust and old paper and stale cigarette-ash.

Outside, too, the City was cheerless. Compared to the rest of the country, the City is like another planet, where plants do not grow and there are only dun colours. You could imagine yourself looking down from above into those streets like narrow desert canyons, at lunchtime say, and seeing simply an enlarged ant's nest.

The City has always had a tradition of independence, *imperium in imperio*, the City state within the nation. Still in the seventeenth century it had its own government (the Corporation), it was walled and fortified, with bands of apprentices trained to arms. With gold in its vaults and direct access to the sea, it could carry on its trading operations without recourse to any authority. It was then, and still is, Mammon's Vatican. And its morality is commercial. Its Bible is the balance sheet. Removed from the actual operation of business, it deals in cyphers only — stocks, securities, contracts, mergers, takeovers, bills, bonds.

It is easier to deal ruthlessly with figures than with people. Lord Chalfont, once Minister of State for Foreign Affairs, recently joined a bank in the City. After less than a year he decided he had had enough. 'Neither the Army nor politics', he said, 'had prepared me for the standards of behaviour I came across in some parts of the City.'

The practice of law is based on principles similar to those of the City. The assumption is that you are not looking to bring about justice yourself, but that if you on your side and another lawyer on the other play every trick you can to further your client's cause, justice will pop out of the middle like a squeezed pip. It may well get to justice as well as any other system, but it does require a quite peculiar style. Lawyers have such a guarded manner.

The law clings to precedent in procedure and language. There are volumes of precedent for every clause of every type of document. Their wording has been tried by the courts and defined. New words would carry the risk of new interpretations. However, the habit affects the whole legal vocabulary, and it gives even contemporary matters an ancient air. Look at Salmond's discussion of *Bourhill v. Young*. With its fish-wife and tramcar, and the motor-car driving 'at an excessive speed', it reads like the record of an Edwardian accident. But the case itself was heard in 1943, and the text of the book was revised in 1953.

I think it was legal language and the legal letter that finally drove me from the law. As an articled clerk one of your few uses to the partners is to draft letters for them to work from. After a while I was able to write a good solicitor's letter, they told me. The secret was to avoid making any assertion of fact whatever. Anything that goes near a direct statement must be qualified with 'it would seem', 'it seems possible that' — or, better still, 'it is not impossible that ...' The ideal letter, either to the client or to the solicitor for the other side, is one that appears to deal with the matter but says nothing at all. The paragraphs are balanced alternately to make it clear that, if from the first one thing seems possible, exactly the opposite could be said to be possible from the second—but neither could be said to be more likely than the other. It's all very well to be able to see all sides, but after a while the habit of qualification and evasiveness, the inability to commit yourself, affects your whole thinking, and you begin to wonder if you will never again write a sentence of plain English. It was like walking over bog-land: there was never firm ground under you.

For the last year of my three-year articles I had known that I should not want to practise. This was probably the first conscious decision about my own career I had ever taken. Perhaps I was waking from that fifteen-year hibernation. I took the coward's way and decided I should at least go on to qualify as a solicitor. But I had a shock. I failed the final exam.

Mr Letts, when I told him, looked at me with an expression of deep disappointment. He did not like to have failures round him. But, 'Don't worry,' he said. 'It's not important.' But actually it was. It was the first exam I had ever failed in my life.

9. *The State of New England*

I am willing to love all mankind *except an American.*

Dr Samuel Johnson (1709-84)

Two empires will divide the world between them—Russia to the East and America to the West. And we, the peoples between these two, will be too discredited, we will have sunk too low, to know except through a vague and incoherent tradition, what we once were.

Friedrich Grimm (1723-1807)

My book rests on the assumption that America—and I would certainly include Britain in this—is the society which works, in which it is possible to participate and do work of integrity while sharing in its material rewards.

Norman Podhoretz, in an interview on publication of *his* autobiography, *Making It*, 1968

American firms operating in this country earn on average almost twice the rate of profit of their British opposite numbers.

Eric Hobsbawm, 1970

Most of what's wrong with today is America. I've got a phobia about it.

Nancy Mitford, 1970

In 1965, in New York, I had dinner with the intellectual Norman kings of the East Coast, Mailer and Podhoretz. That evening on TV Lyndon Johnson was making his first major statement on the war in Vietnam. He certainly had an attentive audience in these two. From the table they sized up the TV set like boxers, jeering, challenging, poking forkfuls of bloody roast beef towards their President's worried face, his serious concerned expression. Norman Mailer was *personally* affronted by the deviousness of Johnson. Norman Podhoretz, with his intellectual's knack of proposing the unexpected, found some sense in what he said, shreds of sympathy, discovering such original reasons for interpreting this or that phrase as a good thing. Both were quick, involved, judging their President with fiery, nervous, subtle processes of mind, ready like jackals to pounce on an unguarded flank.

At the time I knew nothing of the history of that war. I had made no engagement to it that could offer even comment in this keen company, and I remained mostly silent, nervous and restrained. Indeed, they encouraged my participation, but I really did not have a word. For much of the evening I talked on bland topics — acting, painting, travel — to Mailer's calm and pleasantly ironic wife. Later, Norman Mailer joined us and, when he heard us talk of painting, suggested I should go to a friend of theirs who owned a gallery in New York: she could be reckoned to know what was really going on. 'Good,' I said. 'Yes.' 'Here,' Mailer said. He took a book from his pocket and wrote me a note for her.

The note was charming and flattering. And I, as I read it,

said, 'Oh, this is too good to give away.' Mailer turned aside. Kindly, not sharply, with a certain sad frankness, he said, 'Trust an Englishman to spoil it like that.'

Now I take him to be right on every count: right in his judgment, right in his rebuke, right not to suppress it (as most English would) for reasons of politeness. But the story does not end there. The next day, my last in New York, I went to the gallery. They were mounting a new show. The owner was not there. I was really worried by this. What should I do? I had this note. I had rightly been snubbed for suggesting it was too good to hand away. Would Mailer one day ask his friend casually if she had seen this Englishman? And when she told him no, would he think the worst—that I had kept the note for the sake of vanity?

I couldn't risk that. In desperation I asked a girl there—one of those beautiful and super-cool girls they always seem to have in galleries—to pass my note on. I knew it was a pointless gesture. The note was, 'This is to introduce...' What sense could that make without a person behind it? But I also knew that I was not able to walk out of there with that piece of paper in my pocket.

For a long time I was agonized by this small gaucherie, and did not understand the reason. It seemed so unimportant. Yet the embarrassment was a piece that would not pass out of my system. And in time I came to realize why. That scene stood as some sort of culmination to thirty years' education in a British society.

By the standards of the British system, I could have been said to be a success. If I put on a uniform, men saluted me. I could put five letters after my name, awarded by an ancient and famous university. Yet I was not equipped to deal with even the simplest exchanges of human intercourse. And, though I may not be entirely typical, I am not so aberrant that I do not pass for a quite ordinary Englishman. It was English society, not me alone, that chose to avoid the dangers of human contact, to prefer the form to the matter, manners to man. It was not for myself that I was saluted – as we were very often reminded – but for the King's commission I wore on my shoulder. It is, for instance, the fear of an unequivocal encounter with naked humanity that has inhibited even a calm consideration of psychology in this country. We have the best tailors in the world: their art consists in the ability to camouflage.

Everyone imagines they live in times of change. The past and the future divide exactly at the point on which we stand, and naturally we see ourselves at the crossroads. Each generation is in reaction away from its predecessor, and to that extent we are all witnesses to changing times. But equally, succeeding generations are not clear-cut, there is not mass simultaneous childbirth every ten years, and it is impossible to put exact dates on social changes. Much of the education I have experienced and have tried to describe here is twenty years out of date. But the generations do overlap, and the old learn cunning with experience, and cling to power. Nor is change ever as rapid as it seems. The avantgarde makes news; the normal is uninteresting – but more widespread.

Yet change has been, and is taking place, at every level – global, national and personal. It came to the surface in 1956, the year of Budapest, Suez and *Look Back in Anger*. Suez was a British national trauma, a cathartic experience, long overdue, that finally brought home to us this fact: a view of anything has subject and object, which necessarily reflect one another. The object's attitude had changed, but we had failed to notice. Nelson's blind eye is a national impediment (Ireland is its most recent victim). At Suez we were surprised to find that the rest of the world had relegated us to the status of a minor nation that can start a war and not involve the Great Powers.

My whole generation grew up in something of this state of bewilderment. Trained for the hypocrisies of the old society, when we stepped out over the drawbridge we found

we were in a no-man's-land, between the old and the new.
We did not arrive, because there was no place for us.
Neither side would claim us. We had the Janus vision,
looking both ways. The old values, the old judgments by
which we had been taught, still survived, still carried the
greater power. Many of them still prevail. But it was becoming increasingly clear that they were not the as-of-right,
God-given commandments that they claimed to be. We
had nowhere to go, so we melted away. Having no position
as a generation ourselves, we were forced to join one of
the others. We divided. The bright and bold became part of
the younger group. Some became older — even in appearance, some of them — and gave their parents' lives a second
showing. Others suspended animation a while longer, or
for ever.

In New York in the early 'sixties I encountered the
American style, with its vitality, the sophisticated vulgarity,
the sense of engagement. The American dream — as you can
see again from Norman Podhoretz's words — was showing
only initial signs of becoming a nightmare. I was powerfully affected. In that I was merely following, rather late, on
recent European experience. After World War II, and in
the 'fifties particularly, the great Americanization of Europe
took place. It affected our language: our heroes were in the
movies and they spoke American — usually without moving
their lips. It affected our businesses: by 1968, U.S. companies manufactured 10 per cent of British home-produced
goods, held 15 per cent of our bank deposits; of the ten chief
chemical suppliers to the National Health Service, eight
were American-owned; 60 per cent of the British car industry's output came from American-owned firms.* The
younger men eagerly adopted American management
techniques, and the new, post-war salesman appeared —

---

* Not only manufacture is affected. My father's firm now has an agency for
Vauxhall vehicles, and so is tied to General Motors. They are keen to see their agents
practise American methods of competitive management.

impatient, ruthless, immaculately after-shaved, charmingly persuasive. 'If we deprive ourselves', wrote Jean-Jacques Servan-Schreiber in France in 1967, 'of the injection of dynamism, organization, innovation and boldness that characterize the giant American corporations, we will fall even further behind.'

Americanization affected our culture: for the first time we saw the New York school of painting, and the monumental abstracts; American writing sparked with such vitality that English prose by comparison seemed a rigid and stilted language; we believed America had invented a new art form, the musical. American popular music swept our native product out of existence. 'If a people – like the English –' wrote Colin McInnes in 1957, 'sings about another people – the Americans – then this may be a sign that it is ceasing to be a people in any real sense at all.' He could have made the point even more strongly: the English did not only sing about the Americans, they tried to sing as if they *were* Americans.

Just after the second war Lord Keynes was asked if he did not see Britain becoming the forty-ninth United State (as it then would have been). 'No such luck,' he replied. The consumer society certainly tied in with his theories, and at the time seemed also to be proving them correct. In the rhythm of national life-spans – synthesis, expansion, consolidation, decay – Britain had reached the final stage. Our history had trained us for empire, and now, like men reaching retirement, we needed to be retrained for old age. We had put ourselves in pawn for years to pay the expenses of the war, and we looked enviously and rather bitterly at the way the United States was able to afford steaks and expensive toys. We were old, and the U.S.A. was young. They had crudely annexed so much of what we treasured: they had taken the culture we thought was ours and they had perverted it ... It is no easier for nations than for people to forgive one another for being young.

Despite our resentment, we succumbed to Americanization. In the 'sixties we had a brief second childhood: the Beatles wrote songs that showed something like genius, and we produced other talents that made England fashionable for a while. But Americanization continued, and continues. Our joining the Common Market will not affect this, for the whole of Europe is susceptible. Americanization, indeed, has probably brought the countries of Europe closer to one another. Simon and Garfunkel are heard on the Ruhr, and Coke and hamburgers proliferate, even in Paris.

'Perhaps one of the reasons why so many people, even in the Tory party, find his manner unattractive is that he does not behave like the traditional English politician. With his square City double-breasted suits and carefully trimmed, wavy hair he may look English but his style is American.' But Peter Walker, Minister of the Environment — this is the *Sunday Times*'s description — who has built his career on what we have come to call 'American methods' (the chief characteristic of which lies not in being tough, energetic, ruthless, ambitious, but in allowing these qualities to show), is the most successful younger politician of his party. Those 'American methods' are clearly effective for politics and business. But elsewhere the Americanization that affects Europe in the 'seventies is of a slightly different kind. As signs of the failure of the American consumer society become evident and nationality becomes less important an international Western style is arising that Americanizes with more discriminate admiration.

'What is happening in this country among the young,' James Baldwin said recently, 'and not only to the black young, is an overwhelming suspicion that it's not worth it … I mean, I am questioning the values on which society thinks of itself as being based.' Now this, as has been pointed out more than once, * is a version of revolution. Histori-

---

* Even at book length, by Jean-François Revel in *Ni Marx Ni Jésus*, in 1970. 'The revolution of the twentieth century', he writes, 'will take place in the United States.

cally the interesting question is what will happen when these young revolutionaries succeed as rulers. In thirty years the transition will have taken place. Some of them will no doubt grow fat and learn to embrace the the society they are now rejecting. Some are only pretending, playing at revolution. But if sufficient stay faithful to their own creed, even in part, history will want to know if their resources are going to be sufficient to maintain the ascendancy of the United States. Perhaps they will not even desire to do so? And if they do not, shall we—and they—be looking for a lead elsewhere—to China perhaps, or the Third World of Black Africa?

Whatever the eventual outcome, some present change is certain. Much has already taken place. The 'revolution' is American because America is the most powerful force. But a generation exists in England, parallel to and imitative of its American contemporary. It too has broken with Puritan tradition. It is a generation to whom 'Manners Makyth Man' has proved a terrible deception. Its members are therefore suspicious of formality. They cannot comprehend the working of blind patriotism. To them, freemasonry is a fraud. They reject the conception of a master/servant relationship. Socialist peers are ridiculous; so are dancing lessons, and old school ties. They are serious about poetry, but quite uninterested in the idea of a Poet Laureate. They resist the pressures to cleanliness: the plastic doll, Zsa-Zsa Gabor image of glamour has given it a bad name. They do not want status-symbol cars: they would rather have a Volkswagen than a Jaguar. They reject a certain sort of privacy, that covers a fear of inadequacy: they do not think secrets are important, but neither are they curious or prying. They are not concerned with appearances, or compromise. They reject the inhumanity of bureaucracy. They expect teachers to teach students what they want to learn, to co-operate, and listen to criticism, even of themselves. What they want from

---

It could not take place anywhere else. It has already started. And it will only follow in the rest of the world if it is first successful in North America.'

their teachers is straight skills: they prefer to make their own cultural judgments, and not to have the received values handed down. They do not put much store on analysis, or factual investigations that avoid emotional involvement.* Past societies have fought for the freedom to marry for love; now these people have the freedom not to marry. They can draw their myths and their beliefs, not from the Church of England, or Greek culture, but from the whole world: Asian Indian, American Indian, West Indian are equally likely. Their experience of smooth talkers has made them distrust communication, and they are inarticulate. They do not see why they should live by other people's rules, to other people's standards. They ignore national politics: they are interested in wide affairs—which of course provides easy reasons for not taking action.

Many of the attitudes on this somewhat idealized list are inactive, private, in a certain sense anti-social. Yet it's perfectly possible to hold them, and still be able to run the railways, or collect taxes. Not, however, in the style in which these systems are run at present. Nor indeed, within the old type of society—the society for which my education was training me.

Meanwhile, two worlds co-exist, a dual society, two cultures in the same territory, waiting for an outcome. As a country we are deeply in debt, and powerless. A. J. P. Taylor has called our decision to accept lend-lease in 1941 'the most important decision in modern British history'. We had to have the money to fight the war, and Churchill took it without truly understanding that it was not a gift. Some say Roosevelt set it up as a deliberate plan to destroy the wealth and power of the British Empire. Thirty years later, Britain has become a tourist stop on other people's Grand Tour, a restful place to visit; 'an aquatinted country, full of very very nice people, half asleep', it appeared to Alan Pryce-

---

* Even in 1928 E. M. Forster, mystified by T. S. Eliot's *The Waste Land*, asked 'the young' what it was about. They told him, 'It's just a poem.'

Jones in 1968. Three million visitors a year stop over, buy some wild clothes, learn some Cockney rhyming slang, take a trip to Stratford-on-Avon, and depart.

To those visitors we seem calm, honest and exceedingly polite. 'We are English, and that is one good fact,' Oliver Cromwell said to parliament in 1656. John Milton, Cromwell's contemporary, held a similar view: 'Let not England forget her precedence in teaching the natives how to live.' We should have forgotten it sooner.